PAULA PRYKE OBE
Floristry now
FLOWER DESIGN AND INSPIRATION

PAULA PRYKE OBE
Floristry now
FLOWER DESIGN AND INSPIRATION

jacqui
small

First published in 2017 by
Jacqui Small LLP
74–77 White Lion Street
London N1 9PF

Publisher: Jacqui Small
Managing Editor: Emma Heyworth-Dunn
Designer: Maggie Town
Editor: Sian Parkhouse
Production: Maeve Healy

ISBN: 978 1 910254 60 8

A catalogue record for this book is available
from the British Library.

2019 2018 2017
10 9 8 7 6 5 4 3 2 1

Printed in China

Quarto is the authority on a wide range
of topics. Quarto educates, entertains
and enriches the lives of our readers –
enthusiasts and lovers of hands-on living.
www.QuartoKnows.com

Contents

The enduring appeal of flowers

I have been working in the flower industry now for over 30 years, and started my own flower business in 1987. I feel privileged to have found an occupation that I love and to be able to work with the seasonal colour palette of nature. Flowers are central to my life, and whether you work with flowers or not they have the power to lift your spirits and bring colour, beauty and scent to our daily lives. They are often the most emotive gift we give, and they are present at our most important events, from the cradle to the grave. Whether it is growing and tending flowers in the garden or enjoying arranging them for friends, family or just yourself, they have widespread and perennial appeal.

This book is a celebration of floral design and a personal insight to my inspirations. Whether you plan to work with flowers or whether you just enjoy flower arranging in your own home, my advice is to hone your own creativity. Floristry, like fashion, has cycles and trends that appear and reappear, and so this is my personal view of flower design today.

The most wonderful thing about working with flowers is that there is a constantly changing palette to play with. This is in part because of the seasonality of the plant material. But it is also because new cultivars and varieties are constantly being presented in the international flower markets, offering exciting new design opportunities.

The power of flowers is undeniable.

OPPOSITE Who wouldn't feel uplifted by such a pretty combination? 'Lady Bombastic' spray roses, *Viburnum opulus*, and white and pink sweet peas combine with forget-me-nots (*Myosotis sylvatica*). The darker tiny blue flowers are green alkanet (*Pentaglottis sempervirens*), which grows wild in my garden.

Taking inspiration

OPPOSITE Eryngium is becoming an all-year-round flower and 'Sirius', pictured here, is one of the most popular varieties. It has a good metallic colour and adds great texture to designs.

THIS PAGE The giant heads of *Hydrangea arborescens* 'Annabelle' are stunning enough to display simply in vases, accompanied only by single leaves of *Brunnera macrophylla* 'Jack Frost'.

I was inspired to be a florist by the flowers themselves. My environment and early influences in the Suffolk countryside were undoubtedly the seed from where the plant germinated. From that all kinds of other forces have galvanized and energized me, and that in turn has informed my style. Gardens and landscapes, art works and architecture, the interiors of my clients' homes and their desires, product launches, PR events, fashion shows and the city vibe: all have suggested designs to me. My team always inspires me, too. We chat about how best to tackle a new design, the best mechanics, the best combination, or just talk flowers! Working with other talented people is exhilarating. I am an avid book collector and before the internet, I found lots of influences from books. Now we have Pinterest and Instagram for our daily animation. I have worked in many different cultures and countries and this has also had a great influence on me. Keep an open mind, keep up with the new trends, fashions and styles and the inspiration will come to you.

Inspired by nature

Nature is my biggest inspiration and the best teacher. It can be a wild and rugged landscape, a well-designed garden, manicured borders or just simply the plant material itself. There is just such a huge variety of plant material available and always new varieties being offered, that there is always something fresh to consider. Colour, texture and the shape of individual flowers can often inspire my designs. It is important to study the natural world and take inspiration from the seasons.

LEFT Enjoying a moment with the wild meadow buttercups (*Ranunculus acris*) and the common daisies (*Bellis perennis*). Important for pollinating insects, both these 'weeds' are to be encouraged and not mown when in full flower.
OPPOSITE The wild look can be achieved with a mix of garden plants – *Crocosmia* 'Lucifer', *Echinops ritro* 'Veitch's Blue', *Daucus carota* and *Viburnum opulus* berries – with cultivated cut flowers that have 'wild' origins, such as the Raspberry Scoop scabious.

WILD FLOWERS
When I look back on my career I can see the influence of my early life growing up in rural Suffolk. My childhood was spent riding ponies and playing with dogs on water meadows and picking wild flowers on a disused railway line. I still find inspiration in the woods, in the open arable fields and by streams and meadows. The landscape and the revolving seasons constantly stimulate new ideas or thoughts. A lot of flowers we love in the wild, such as bluebells, campanula and achillea, have been cultivated and are now widely available as cut flowers, so we can leave wild flowers in their natural habitat where they belong! Primroses and cowslips are sold as plants and can also be used in cut flower designs or potted arrangements. Added to this there are lots of foliages and branches we can use from the wild, such as the common ivy berries or the more exotic spindle berry. The wide-scale production of berries, hips and seedheads also is testament to how strong the trend is for the wild-flower look.

LEFT A Raku vase is filled with poppy seedheads, *Daucus carota*, the field scabious (*Knautia arvensis*), *Solidaster luteus, Echinops bannaticus* 'Blue Pearl', *Anethum graveolens*, lavender, *Panicum* 'Fountain', *Astrantia* 'Roma', *Achillea major* 'Claret' and common knapweed (*Centaurea nigra*).

THIS PAGE Pooley vases hold poppy seedheads, *Daucus carota*, *Achillea millefolium*, *Anethum graveolens*, *Panicum* 'Fountain', *Achillea major* 'Claret', *Centaurea nigra*, *Filipendula ulmaria*, hogweed (*Heracleum spondylium*), scentless mayweed (*Tripleurospermum inodorum*), fennel (*Foeniculum vulgare*), wild parsnip (*Pastinaca sativa* ssp. *sylvestris*) and prickly sow thistle (*Sonchus asper*).

LEFT *Lavandula angustifolia.*
'Hidcote' is one of my favourite
lavender varieties because of
its dark colour.
RIGHT I decorated a glass
vase with trimmed stems of
'Hidcote' lavender, attached with
double-sided tape and tied with
seagrass. The summery bouquet
includes *Thlaspi* 'Green Trick',
Champney's Pink Cluster and
Titanic roses, *Astrantia major*
'Roma', *Alchemilla mollis* and
Achillea millefolium 'Masterclass'.

SUMMER LAVENDER With the wide-scale production of flowers through

the world, there are a lot of flowers that are available through the year. This makes flowers that are seasonal even more enticing to use in their short but brief season. Lavender is a nostalgic flower, most people can identify it and most love the scent. It is relatively easy and fast to grow and thrives in a sunny border. As well as being decorative it can be used as a culinary herb, and the essential oil has anti-inflammatory and antiseptic qualities. A cultivated field of lavender is a beautiful sight – and a lovely scent – to behold. As lavender tends to get lost in mixed arrangements I like to use it as part of the container, either held on by double-sided tape around a glass vase (as shown opposite) or tied or wired into a basket with rafia or stub wires (see also pages 240–45). The other way I use lavender is bunched simply and pinned into designs. It looks best upright, resembling its natural growing pattern – so much can be learnt about good floral design from observing plants in their natural habitat. There are many lavender farms in the United Kingdom, especially local to me in Norfolk, but the place to go to be truly inspired by lavender is Provence. From June to August you can visit the Luberon around Mont-Ventoux, Sault and Valréas and see the lavender fields. Stop at the Lavender Museum in Coustellet to see just how inspirational this legendary flower has been.

SINGLE COLOURS

Lavender is not the only flower that inspires me en masse. Any flower field of one colour shows how impactful a monochromatic flower scheme can be. Translated into flower design, the simplicity of one colour can look amazing on the spot-lit tabletops of a huge ballroom. It can be a layer of white snowdrops in the early part of the year, or a carpet of bluebells in an ancient woodland in April and May. In June, it is very often the sight of red poppies that have germinated profusely on poor soil. In the Keukenhof gardens in the Netherlands they plant swathes of one-colour bulbs every spring – also a huge source of inspiration. Flowering crops such as linseed and rapeseed demonstrate the different effects of a single colour. You see how the blue of linseed recedes, whereas the bright yellow rapeseed advances. Another flower field crop that inspires me is sunflowers. During growth the flowers track the sun's direction – this tendency is called heliotropism. The sight of these tall flowers all pointing in the same direction is magical. Although I love to mix colour I never underestimate the power of a single colour to arrest and lift spirits.

OPPOSITE *Echinops bannaticus* 'Blue Pearl' and *Echinops ritro* 'Veitch's Blue' are massed on a floral foam ring. The subtly contrasting shades give depth and texture.

LEFT In these ancient bluebell woods at Gaynes Park in Essex, masses of *Hyacinthoides non-scripta* flower at once, giving a breathtaking display. The scent, captured beneath the trees, is also a bonus.

LEFT A mature oak grows beside a field of the intense yellow blooms of rapeseed. Observing the growth pattern gives me insight into how to arrange branches and stems in a vase so they look natural.

OPPOSITE Winter white amaryllis have been arranged with leafless Japanese magnolia stems in a glass vase filled with floral foam concealed by sand and delicate coral fern.

THE SEASONS Seasonal change is a very important influence on my work, particularly the observation of the shape of deciduous trees and bushes. Naked trees in winter show their structure and many branch patterns demonstrate how stems and branches should be arranged in a large vase or urn. Winter is also a good time for seeing how foliage can work in flower arrangements. In the summer you hardly notice the evergreens, but in winter they take on a new appeal. The holly looks glossy and the ivy has an interesting vein structure plus beautiful berries. The silver spruces and grey rosemary and eucalyptus take on a more important role in the winter months. Most of the year I am not at all keen on variegated foliage unless it is used in white and green designs. However, in the winter I am drawn to them to add colour to my designs. The use of foliage and branches is very crucial to the English style of flower arranging, and so it has always been a big part of my floral designs. In a mixed arrangement I like to use at least three types of greenery to make it look more natural. In the spring it might be blossom, in the summer it will be something wild and natural and possibly grasses, and in the autumn berries and seedheads. The English tradition of flower arranging has always championed the all-green arrangement, so much so that flower growers have created a green palette of flowers. From lime green Kangaroo paw, *Anigozanthos flavidus*, right through to the green *Zinnia* 'Envy' there are green varieties to be found in almost every plant family.

Inspired by art and design

Art has always been a huge influence on my work and many different movements and genres have provided ideas for my floral design. About the most obvious is the Dutch and Flemish movement in the 17th and 18th centuries. My first exposure to this genre was when a Flemish aunt gave an amateur version of this style of painting to my parents and it was hung in pride of place on the mantelpiece!

LEFT In *A Vase of Flowers*, 1663, by Willem Aelst, typical of the Dutch Golden Age of painting, you can really appreciate the forms and combinations of the flowers.
RIGHT In my interpretation of this style, this oil pot from Provence is filled with foxgloves and coral and red peonies, mixed with dark purple *Prunus* and the dangly explosions of fountain grass. The grass softens the arrangement and the flowers and foliage are in harmony with the vase. I find that this kind of classic arrangement will suit traditional spaces and soften more contemporary interiors.

OLD MASTERS
The Dutch and Flemish masters were inspired by the exciting new plants and bulbs being introduced to their generation. These 17th-century paintings encapsulated the fervour and reverence that exotic flowers were causing in Europe. This later became known as the 'Golden Age' of flower painting. Flowers that were not indigenous to Europe, such as opium poppies, tulips, crown imperials and madonna lilies, were introduced in the second half of the 16th century and they caused quite a stir. Tulips, in particular, became so popular that their value rose astronomically until 1637, when a buyer from Haarlem did not show up to pay for his bulb purchases and the panic caused a crash. Our economic crashes since the 17th century have not been so directly linked to flowers, but the economy does affect the flower and plant industry markedly. During downturns we return to a more nostalgic and romantic look, whereas in times of strength floral boundaries are tested and pushed more.

LEFT *Sunflowers*, 1889, Vincent van Gogh. The rough beauty, distinct brushstrokes and the bold use of colour had far-reaching effects on 20th-century art.
OPPOSITE 'Teddy Bear' sunflowers, a modern variety, have the same density of petals. Here thay are mixed with *Viburnum opulus* berries.

THE IMPRESSIONISTS
Later, in the 19th century, botanical adventurers who were bringing exotic plants from China and Japan influenced art. The impressionists sought not to make accurate copies of nature but impressions. Monet's famous paintings of his garden at Giverny are so inspirational for their colours alone. Monet, arguably one of the most significant painters of the garden, said he owed his painting 'to flowers'. The garden was an inspiration to Renoir, Cezanne and Matisse, and in turn their work inspires and informs my designs. Vincent van Gogh started to paint flowers in 1884 with *Vase with Honesty*. He wrote: 'I have lacked money for models…but I have made a series of colour studies in painting simple flowers, red poppies, blue cornflowers and myosotis.' After a visit to Arles in the South of France he took to sunflowers, and after a traumatic episode he ended up in an asylum in Saint-Remy, where he painted irises. His most famous flower paintings come from the end of his life. In the same way that the artists were inspired by the new flowers, florists are inspired by the new varieties that are developed each season. This gives us an ever-evolving palette of colours and textures to work with.

LEFT Constance Spry designed her own range of vases in the mid 1930s and these were made for her by the Fulham Pottery in west London. The Pottery followed these with further ranges designed by their in-house designer WJ Marriner and by Gerard de Witt, as were these vases from the 1930s.
OPPOSITE The garden was an important source for Constance Spry's arrangements, as it is for me. These garden pickings include pinks, *Prunus* 'Royal Burgundy', American pokeweed (*Phytolacca americana*), Cecile Brunner shrub roses, pink *Lathyrus ororatus* 'Banty' and the everlasting sweet pea *Lathyrus grandiflorus*.

CONSTANCE SPRY
The famous British author, educator and florist was best known for arranging the flowers for Queen Elizabeth's coronation in 1953. She opened her first shop in 1928, called Flower Decoration, and wrote her first book with the same title in 1934. Later she went on to establish a domestic science school at Winfield Place in Berkshire. When I was deciding to change careers from teaching history to secondary school pupils, I enrolled on a Constance Spry flower arranging course in my long summer vacation. Constance had died at Winfield in 1960, the year I was born. However, the staff who remained at the school remembered her very fondly in 1985 when I was a pupil, and they referred to her as Mrs Spry as if she was omnipresent. Constance could see the value of flower arranging to ordinary people who were living in austere conditions following the Second World War. She championed the use of arranging one thing in a vase, such as lilac, and keeping it simple. She also encouraged people to think about using kale and items from the vegetable patch in their arrangements. Her arrangements were natural and she encouraged the use of wild flowers and sprigs from the hedgerow. She wrote many books on flower design and lectured in the United States as well as at home and was the single most important figure in floristry and floral design in the 20th century.

THIS PAGE This Fulham Pottery vase design – the FMA – was used frequently by Constance Spry. In tribute to her I've filled one with Constance Spry, Classic Kate, Dorothy Perkins, Savoy Gardens, Carey and Romantic roses, *Achillea millefolium* 'Paprika', valerian (*Valeriana officinalis*), agrimony (*Agrimonia eupatoria*), tufted vetch (*Vicia cracca*), everlasting sweet pea, (*Lathyrus grandiflorus*), loosestrife, (*Lysimachia ciliata* 'Firecracker'), borage (*Borago officinalis*), *Daucus carota*, *Chasmanthium latifolium*, perennial cornflower (*Centaurea montana*), *Thlaspi* 'Green Bell', dill (*Anethum graveolens*), violets, canterbury bells (*Campanula medium*), clematis trails, the variegated leaves of *Brunnera macrophylla* 'Jack Frost' and branches of small green apples.

GRAPHIC ART
Another art form that has influenced some of my work
is the graphic forms of the 20th-century modern art movement, those based more
on line and colour. There is lots to be learnt about using blocks, groups or swathes
of colour from these art works. Non-representational art has a purity of form that
allows you to concentrate on the colours and their effects. You can really appreciate
how one colour alters the strength of another colour simply by being placed next
to it. The works of Piet Mondrian, for example, started by being inspired by the
landscape but ended up being grid-based, very abstract representations of the
spiritual order underlying the visible world. For me, Paul Klee is also a very interesting
artist and he wrote and thought a lot about colour theory. He had been inspired
by Robert Delaunay's bold use of colour. Henri Matisse also produced very bright
and inspirational colour themes. He said, 'It is not enough to place colours, however
beautiful, one beside the other; colours must also react on one another. Otherwise,
you have cacophony.' This is equally applicable in garden design and flower arranging.

Inspired by trends

Fashion is in love with flowers at the moment; flowers are sexy again. Floral prints are enjoying a revival, and colour trends convince growers to invest in new varieties, so the colour palette of cut flowers is continuously evolving. Trends in gardening also influence production. Plants prevalent in the show gardens of garden design shows soon appear in gift bouquets and flower decorations.

LEFT English seasonal hydrangeas with a small selection of my arsenal of jugs, vases, pots, urns, bottles and vessels for flower arranging on any scale. **OPPOSITE AND OVERLEAF** Jugs always look in style. This enamel pitcher is filled with a glorious mix of *Alchemilla mollis*, 'Blackbery Scoop' scabious, sweet peas, fountain grass, *Thlaspi perfoliatum* 'Green Bell', *Daucus carota*, valerian, cotinus, viburnum berries, *Achillea millefolium* 'Pink Grapefruit' and Wedding Bells, Combo and pink standard Titanic roses.

VINTAGE I have always felt a strong connection with the past and grew up in a small medieval town in a district with many antiques shops. The East Anglia of my childhood was steeped in medieval history, and consequently history was my favourite subject at school and I went on to study it at university. When I studied floristry at the Constance Spry school, there was a big connection with the heritage and antiquities that Mrs Spry had amassed over the years. When I began my interest in floral design, Kenneth Turner was the top London flower decorator. He had a flower shop in Mayfair with an Islington antiques dealer called Keith Skeel, and it was so perfect to see these wonderful flower arrangements in antique urns and pots. The used and weathered pots told a story, and the recycling of old items mirrors the rebirth of nature each year. The influence of the past dips in and out of fashion, but we all get some inspiration from what has gone before us and it informs our creative processes.

OPPOSITE In 1965, a British engineer called Denys Fisher invented the best design tool ever – the Spirograph! It was the most exciting invention, allowing me to create colourful patterns and flower shapes. Interestingly, some of those graphic patterns can be seen in flower heads such as daisies, sunflowers and dahlias. Portmerion pottery produces this jug, called Crazy Daisy, which reminds me of the swinging sixties, when I would sit for hours making colourful patterns with my Spirograph. These multicoloured gerbera daisies also hark back to that flower power era.

RIGHT The gerbera has come a long way from its origins in the Transvaal desert of South Africa. Through amazing breeding and hybridizing it is available in a range of sizes, shapes and an enormous number of colours. I love to use the clashing colours of new varieties such as 'Tesla' and 'Pink Springs' with textural umbels of *Daucus carota, Anethum graveolens,* cotinus and *Viburnum opulus* berries.

FLOWER POWER I was born in 1960. One of my earliest family memories was sitting between my two brothers in the back of a car listening to Frank and Nancy Sinatra, who were top of the charts with 'Somethin' Stupid'. That year was 1967, the summer of love. The Flower Power era of the 1960s started as a protest against the Vietnam War, but became part of the popular culture in the following decade. The psychedelic art, the graphics and the vibrant colours, along with the protest songs of Bob Dylan and the intriguing album covers for the Beatles, were the soundtrack of my first decade. In my teens, the glam rock and blurring of artistic lines by heroes such as David Bowie were inspiring. Flowers symbolized peace, freedom, rebellion and youth. The fantasy art works and the colourful fashion of this period definitely influenced my love of colour. The tie-dye clothes, colourful beads and embroidered Afghan coats were so exotic.

JAPANESE STYLE
Shortly after my first book was published in 1993, I received calls from Japan and the USA to demonstrate my floral style. I took four trips to Japan in the 1990s and it is such an inspirational country to visit. The contradiction between a country that is steeped in tradition but embraces fashion and technology is fascinating. The Japanese form of flower arranging, Ikebana, is an exploration of simplicity and the reverence of the single flower or bloom. They make the best pin holders, the sharpest knives and superlative floristry tools. They produce fabulous pottery and I am a huge fan of Raku ware, the distinctive fired stoneware pots. The Japanese are also known for beautiful handmade papers, and they have a dedication to excellence and reverence for master craftsmen of all fields that is very refreshing. Alongside the Dutch, they are also very talented at producing wonderful cut flowers. Their production of ranunculus, sweet peas and gloriosa is outstanding. They also specialize in *Tweedia caerulea*. Japan is simply unique and very stimulating to visit.

ABOVE LEFT Japanese pottery with small pin holders displaying grasses, *Sanguisorba officinalis* and Japanese anemones.
ABOVE RIGHT *Clematis rehderiana* and bun moss remind me of some of the sensitive planting in Japanese gardens. The Japanese adore this very floriferous and beautiful bell-shaped clematis.
OPPOSITE Simplicity, balance and the importance of composition are lessons I take from Japanese art. Here, a moon vase holds red Vanda orchids, green Phornium leaves and trimmed lengths of red bamboo.

LEFT For me, a defining feature of Scandinavian design is clarity of line. Displaying plants and flowers individually allows you to appreciate their form. This group is of white alliums, the seedheads of Solomon's seal, forest fern (*Dryopteris filix-mas*) and scentless mayweed (*Tripleurospermum maritimum*).

OPPOSITE This simple approach to floristry really suits modern living. Here forest fern and Solomon's seal are joined by 'Kobe' phalaenopsis orchids in the large pot, white 'Annabelle' hydrangeas and delicately veined leaves from *Brunnera macrophylla* 'Jack Frost'.

SCANDI STYLE
Living with an architect for the last three decades I have an appreciation for classic Scandinavian design, from Arne Jacobsen and Alvar Aalto to Marimekko. The Nordic countries have an unpretentious approach to design. Furniture is useful, clean lined and made often from natural, plain materials such as wood, sheepskin, wool and leather. Design, in the Scandinavian tradition, provides emotional comfort and enriches daily life. It mixes practical and traditional craftsmanship with products from the natural world. The region's endless dark winters might have influenced the style. In 1919, Gregor Paulsson, who was then Director of the Swedish Design Council, said he admired products that 'lend grace to the chore of life'. The Scandinavian emphasis on quality and the reverence for individual craftsmen is refreshing, and their relationship with the natural world and the simplicity of their design appeals to me. Swedish fabrics and Scandinavian prints are often inspired by the natural landscape and they give me fresh vision and clarity. Scandinavian floristry is often more about form and structure than the flowers themselves, but their love of nature is always at the heart of it.

Interpreting design

Creativity in the new Pinterest age has been strangely stalled rather than increased by all the visual images now on display. I find that clients now tend to present a collection of images they like rather than have a discussion, so I think there is less room for interpretation, and more copying of images. I think it means that there is less pronounced personal floral style and we all end up working in much the same way. It takes a lot to stand out with your own personal statement and be truly original. If something is hard to make work or look good, walk away from it. You have to feel happy about the work you create and be true to your own aesthetic. The best work is always achieved when you have the confidence to add your own twist and interpretation.

OPPOSITE Props can suggest a design approach: for this wedding, filled vintage port bottles were nestled among lengths of ivy, small green apples and the long tendrils of *Gloriosa superba* 'Sparkling Stripe'.
THIS PAGE Three different varieties of crab apples give variation of colour in a stemmed cookie jar. The lid has been turned upside down to hold a late-summer mix of dahlias, physalis, *Anethum graveolens*, rudbeckia, mini sunflowers, sedum and the pumpkin berries *Auranticarpa rhombifolia*.

PREVIOUS PAGES The brown flocked twigs in this table arrangement are mitsumata *(Edgeworthia chrysantha)* from Japan. They are sold bare or stripped, to add texture to a flower design.

Shape

There are three factors that underlie all good floral designs: form, colour and composition are key. We have discussed how shape and form may be influenced by observing nature. Shape and form are also determined by budget, and possibly the occasion and the location. The first thought process when thinking about the shape is where it will be placed and how it will be viewed. Is it viewed in the round or is he arrangement set against a wall? In my work I like the natural or holistic style – flowers are arranged as if they were growing, and the overall form follows the shape of flowers and branches. This works well for flowers placed on windows or mantelpieces, or small displays on tables.

Massed flowers can be round or linear. The massed shape is very European in its origins. Line arrangements are much looser and use less plant material. They have their origins in Ikebana from Japan. The current shape that is very popular is massed flowers, loosely arranged with not too much symmetry. Structural shapes or simple shapes can be natural and loose, or quite restrained and ordered.

OPPOSITE A simple vase of long-lasting amaryllis flowers is given a more dynamic form with the addition of spiky twigs. I chose these branches because they look aged and interesting. They are from an alder tree found in the hedgerow that separates my garden from that of my neighbours. I also adore old fruit trees for this kind of look as they have very curved branches.

Texture

Along with colour, texture is most important to me as a floral designer. I often think of creating a patchwork of texture when I put together a flower design. Texture gives your composition depth, it makes it tactile and inviting. The right textures make an arrangement look very natural, as there is so much diversity of texture in the natural world. If you just think about the diversity in flower shapes you realize the scale of the possibilities. When you place plant material together, you get a contrast from the positioning. If it is a large-scale piece, you need to select textures and shapes that are very different to achieve a good-looking form. If it is a smaller design, you might think more of using your foliage for the texture, to make the flowers stand out their best. Texture affects colour and should always be considered in relation to colour choices.

OPPOSITE White scabious, poppy seedheads, ivy berries, garden roses, *Alchemilla mollis*, white hydrangea heads and *Ammi visnaga* offer a wealth of frilly, fluffy and smooth, silky textures. Using fruits, such as these small green apples, is a great way to add interest to glass containers,

Scale

The scale of the flowers depends on what you want to achieve with the design. Any assessment of scale means ensuring the arrangement is in proportion to its surroundings, but also applies to the scale of the flowers to the container they are to be placed in. Originally the idea of pleasing proportions came from the Greeks, and over time rules laid down for flower arranging suggested that the flowers should be one and a half times larger than the container. Although this benchmark works it can be misleading if applied too rigidly to all flower design; other proportions also work. If creating a pedestal on a plinth, for example, it is important that the flowers are in proportion to the overall size of the container, the supporting column and the room space.

OPPOSITE This imposing arrangement is composed of an elegant urn-shaped vase, a pronounced dome – created from mixed Black Baccara, All 4 Love+, Marie-Claire!, Ocean Song, Purple Power and Cool Water roses, studded with ming (or asparagus) fern and *Viburnum opulus* – and branches of magnolia offer added stature.

Colour

This for me is the most motivating force of working with nature. Colour in nature is part of the grand design to attract the attention of insects, birds and animals for the pollination and fertilization of the plant kingdom. Some floral designers have a natural talent for colour and colour combinations. Others learn good combinations and safe colour coordination before becoming brave enough to experiment. Colour is very often the first instruction you receive from a client, and the starting point for a design. White and green is always seen as chic and I think this is the 'little black dress' of the flower industry – it is a reliable option and looks good in any environment. Despite the increased use of colour in weddings generally, white and green still dominates ceremony flowers.

Within colour there is much to consider. Harmonious colours work well together, complementary colours are always a good area to start as a novice flower arranger. (See the chapter *Thinking about colour* for more on this.) Contrasting and clashing colours are more difficult to pull off and one needs clever use of foliage and texture to make these work. Monochromatic colours and analogous combinations are also very safe options for the beginner. Understanding and using colour gives me the most joy in my work and I am always learning in this area.

RIGHT Nature is an infallible guide when it comes to colour. Here spring yellows, blues and whites combine in tiny bouquets of *Muscari* 'Bluefields Beauty', *Viola*, 'Carlton' and 'Geranium' narcissus and *Leucojum aestivum*. They look great individually, and even nicer grouped in a wreath-shaped clear glass bowl.

Creating a style

PREVIOUS PAGES The gorgeous soft pink and lemon 'Papiljo' lily is arranged with Sudoku roses, *Molucella laevis*, *Viburnum opulus* blossom, arching stephanandra, variegated trails of ivy and green trailing amaranthus. This graceful combination is a classic for weddings in particular.

THIS PAGE Nature's bounty celebrated and enriched: exotic pink and green celosia, groups of roses, textural orange pin cushion proteas and just a few stems of precious gloriosa have been added to autumnal flowers. Rose hips nestle against orange carthamnus, while bundles of ivy and hypericum berries add structure.

OPPOSITE This rich mix includes *Celosia* 'Bombay Purple', Germini gerbera 'Scream', *Leonotis leonurus*, combined with *Physalis alkekengi*, the burgundy *Dahlia* 'Arabian Night', ivy berries and the pink snowberry *Symphoricarpos* from my garden. Halved aubergines slide over the edges of the heather-covered pot.

Contemporary floristry since the end of the 20th century has undergone a major change. The industry is much more in tune with fashion, interior design and architecture than it ever was before. The party and event industry, plus the dominance of social media, have made trends much more pronounced and copied and, strangely, originality has been stifled. But, from time to time, one predominant fashion dictates a pervasive style, and at the moment I feel we are going through a very romantic, natural period. Wedding work, which is often more formal, still requires more classical design, and sometimes the circumstances or the clients demand a classical shape. Structured work is often more popular in corporate commissions, artistic installations and sometimes parties and events, where the colour is often the focus, too. There has also been a trend to create a mass with lots of flowers, to surprise guests with opulence. So we can see two quite opposing styles operating at the same time: the natural, organic and simple design, against an opulent, massed and sometimes very formal presentation of the natural world. I'm looking at representations of these in this chapter.

Wild

We are all drawn to nature's free bounty and as a consequence many growers have developed over time more 'weedy' looking flowers. People have sought out an alternative to the common all-year-round flowers, which have travelled two weeks by air cargo or three weeks in dry ice in a metal container from China. So the wild-flower craze is in part a reaction to the success of the world flower trade! In the London flower market you can buy foraged flowers from estates that are sent into the foliage departments, and so it was always possible to order cow parsley, wild angelica, guelder roses, fennel and lots of other native weeds. The clever flower and foliage growers all over the world have also cultivated wild-like flowers to meet this demand, such as shepherd's-purse, *Capsella bursa-pastoris*, with heart-shaped seed pods up the stem and *Thlaspi perfoliatum* 'Green Bell', grown in Israel.

LEFT Everlasting sweet pea, feverfew, blackberry, valerian, wild teasels, cow parsley, sweet cicely, pink veronica and musk mallow are each given their own milk bottle vase, and the collection is bound together with gardener's twine.

OPPOSITE Earthenware jars are filled with hand-tied bouquets of eryngium, marguerite daisies, achillea, white commercially grown *Scabiosa caucasiea* var. *alba* with wild *Scabiosa columbaria* and wild knapweed and fresh green wheat, alongside artichokes hollowed out and filled with a pillar candle.

Wild-flower bowl

I grow my own little wild-flower patch at the bottom of my garden in Suffolk. It backs onto a wheat field, and I have added a few ears of wheat to this arrangement as a tribute to the errant cereal plants that stray into my garden. The long, hollow spotted stems used as the base and support for this design were purchased from the Dutch auctions, and are a type of knotweed called *Polygonum persicaria*. It is a great plant for natural designs, and popular in Europe, where this knotweed grows widely.

You will need

10 stems of *Polygonum persicaria*

a selection of wild flowers or small-headed garden flowers: I used echinops, *Daucus carota*, *Campanula rotundifolia*, green alkanet (*Pentaglottis sempervirens*), the common knapweed (*Centaurea nigra*), rosebay willow herb (*Chamerion angustifolium*), field scabious (*Knautia arvensis*), *Achillea millefolium* and wild teasels (*Dipsacus fullonum*)

a straight-sided glass bowl

a strong pair of sharp floristry scissors or secateurs

1 Cut the knotweed down into short lengths so it is flush with the top of the glass dish, taking care to leave some longer side shoots to rise up higher than the bowl.

2 Continue until the knotweed is snug in the bowl and then add some water so the flowers can drink immediately as you position them. Wild flowers do not like to be placed in floral foam and so this design is ideal for adding structure and support to soft plant material. The side shoots help hold everything in place.

3 Start with the more hardy and firm flowers first, and create a structure of different head shapes. Move the bowl around so you work on all sides, and save some of the naturally drooping flowers for the edge of the bowl.

4 Continue until the bowl is full. Fill up to the rim of the glass with water mixed with flower food.

From the garden

Garden flowers, seasonally arranged, are always in vogue. The heritage of the quintessential English garden means that our flower-arranging tradition is rich with plant material. It is no coincidence that British gardens look their best at the end of May when the Royal Horticultural Society holds the famous annual Chelsea Flower Show in London. It is one of my favourite times of the year, as late spring collides with early summer. Garden roses have been one of the areas that has seen an enormous change in the last decade. Originally garden roses were hard to get out of season but over time countries such as Kenya in Africa and Colombia in South America have invested in a lot of garden rose production. Many are the famous roses of the breeder David Austin, and the company have also invested more recently in cut-flower production alongside their plant-growing activities.

ABOVE A pastel watering can is crammed with a selection of spring flowers, including arching Solomon's seal, magnolia buds, lilac, 'Antique' carnations, eryngium, rosebuds and *Viburnum opulus*.

OPPOSITE This fine-looking *Stachys byzantina* is tied to a metal basket with raffia. Floral foam holds 'Miss Delilah' phlox, 'Figaro Lavender' stocks and purple summer asters. Stems of handsome leafless Solomon's seal are then drawn across the design to show off their creamy white bells to maximum effect.

THIS PAGE It is very fashionable to have collections of vases together, with small arrangements or even single stems in each. This makes the maximum impact out of the fewest flowers, so is perfect for making the most of garden pickings. Sprigs of flowering currant, forsythia, viburnum blossom, primroses, hellebores and dicentra sit in tiny irregular vases.
OPPOSITE I love the shape of this enamel jug which, when filled, has a wide enough mouth to create a good spread of flowers. Here it holds *Alchemilla mollis*, *Consolida ajacis*, rose-coloured eustoma, two-tone antirrhinum and the wonderful scented garden rose Evelyn.

Garden flowers hand-tied

This bunch includes some of my favourite cottage garden flowers and one in particular – the bright and cheerful cornflower. *Centaurea cyanus* is a native UK flower that once grew vigorously through summer crops in my home county of Suffolk. When farmers began using herbicides, they started to disappear in the wild. Luckily they flourish in gardens. They are easy to grow from seed, attract pollinating insects and they flower all summer. They're a great cut-and-come again cut flower, with an eye-catching colour.

You will need

a bunch of *Achillea millefolium* 'Paprika'

a bunch of *Anethum graveolens*

5 stems of *Thlaspi perfoliatum* 'Green Bell'

10 stems of *Monarda didyma* 'Pink Lace'

15 stems of *Scabiosa caucasica* 'Lisa'

10 stems of *Veronicastrum virginicum* 'Fascination'

10 stems of *Echinops ritro* 'Veitch's Blue'

a bunch of *Centaurea cyanus*

a rustic oil jar

a roll of bind wire

a strong pair of sharp floristry scissors or secateurs

1 Clean all the leaves from the lower half of the stems. I just slide it off with my hands but you may want to use surgical gloves. Place each variety in its own pile so you can mix the flowers up as you build up your bunch.

2 In your left hand place one central flower and then five further stems to the left of the first one, at an angle of around 15°. When you have a fan of flowers use your right hand to twist them round, then add another 5 stems of plant material. Relax your hand, twisting as you add stems and working slightly lower as the bunch increases, to create a domed effect.

3 When you have added all the plant material, tie with bind wire where you have been holding the bunch: this is the point from where the flowers spiral outwards. Trim to fit your vessel, and fill it with water and flower food. Cottage garden flowers drink heavily, so re-cut the stems, top up the water and refresh with flower food every two to three days.

THIS PAGE Large star-shaped cream 'Concordia' lilies with tall branches of forsythia and foxgloves give height. Huge heads of hydrangea, coral peonies and chrysanthemums make a good impact and look appropriate in the sturdy verdigris urn. The fountain grass and cream hypericum provide a soft edge around the urn and add downward proportion.

Classic

ABOVE This domed orange pedestal has a foliage base of *Sambucus nigra* 'Black Lace', cotinus, *Viburnum opulus* berries and a touch of ivy berries. The roses are Summerhouse roses from VIP growers in the Netherlands, and are a mixture of London Eye and Victorian Peach, with some Caruluna and Orange Romantic.

This design is usually signifed by the type of flower used and the container. Some classic styles that have been traditionally taught to floristry students are now mainly used by flower clubs for competition pieces, but rarely used in the commercial world. These include the asymmetrical triangle, the downward or upward crescent and the Hogarth curve, which loosely follows the line of an S. These have been largely rejected by contemporary floral artists because of their stiffness. The most important classical designs in commercial floristry, and the ones I use the most, are pedestal or urn arrangements, commonly chosen for ceremonies or large gatherings. Dome-shaped table urns are formal, and mantelpiece arrangements can be made in a classical form. The familiar wreath shape and standard balls, whether used as topiary or hanging, are in the same tradition.

Summer glory

For larger classical arrangements it is important to use tall and large-headed flowers to keep the arrangement in porportion to the vase or, in this case, an urn. This urn has been given a modern twist – the overall shape and silhouette are traditional, but it is made from green glass, which gives a contemporary feel. A collar of foliage echoes the rounded bulge of the urn and provides a strong visual link between flowers and container.

1

2

You will need

10 stems of white delphinium

10 stems of white calla lilies

10 stems of Avalanche+ roses

10 stems of white 'Pompei' lilies

8 stems of *Viburnum opulus* 'Roseum'

8 stems of molucella

8 stems of *Syringa* 'Madame Florent Stepman'

10 stems of white larkspur

8 stems of antirrhinums

10 stems of lime green kangaroo paw (*Anigozanthos flavidus*)

a bunch of trailing smilax (*Asparagus asparagoides*)

a large vase

string or floral tie

a strong pair of sharp floristry scissors or secateurs

1 Strip all the lower foliage from the stems so that half of the stem is completely clean and free from any debris. Lay out all your flowers of each variety and then start by taking the first central flower between your thumb and first finger and add 5 pieces of plant material at right angles to the first piece and then twist in your hand. Add another 5 and twist again and continue adding and twisting until you have a well-balanced natural bouquet. Tie firmly with string or floral tie. Trim the ends of the stems with a diagonal cut.

2 Fill the vase with water mixed with flower food. Place the bouquet in the centre of the vase. Untie the tie to loosen the stems a little. Place one end of the smilax into the water and trail the other end around the edge of the vase to create a natural collar.

LEFT Packing plant material tightly can create its own rigidity and overall shape. I adore these Gertrude Jekyll roses mixed with Prima Donna and Super Green roses, sprigs of lime-green *Alchemilla mollis*, pale blue nigella, candy pink nerines, campanula and 'Sarah Bernhardt' peonies.
OPPOSITE This 'cage' is made of white-tinged sorbus branches, just about to burst with their lovely soft green leaves. Long French peach tulips emphasize the structure and soft-petalled peach roses line the base of floral foam at the top of the mossed basket.

Structured

These arrangements either rely on a framework – whether that be a natural structure or mechanics fashioned by the floral artist – or the flowers themselves create a structural look. Continental European floristry and competition floristry is often quite concerned with creating structures. For the most part my structured arrangements are for corporate floristry and contract work. Certain types of flowers, particularly tropical flowers, suit structured work, and branches, berries and strong foliage shapes are perfect. One might be drawn to create more structural works by the demands of certain flowers, such as long, leggy and elegant flowers like French tulips, agapanthus or calla lilies. The current trend for structural designs is much lighter and looser than in previous years. It is possible to create light structural designs by using grasses or bamboo for the structure, and then filling in with wild and garden material, with its imperfections and irregularities.

Structured gerberas

Gerbera United are a Dutch company with the vision to breed and produce new and unique gerberas. Their Ambition specials feature spidery-looking gerberas – some were originally called Pasta and some Springs. For this I chose to use their Pink Springs, Orange Springs and the red Pasta Romana varieties. I adore the intense colour of gerberas and over 30 years they have appeared in many of my designs. Now I mostly include them in gift work and contract work, but their colour range makes them useful when flower supply is not so plentiful – they can make a huge impact in autumn and winter. In the main I am a black centre fan, and tend to specify varieties with black eyes.

You will need

20–25 stems of Pink Springs, Orange Springs and Red Romana gerberas

3 bunches of grey-flocked *Mitsumata* branches

a small bag of Spanish moss (*Tillandsia usneoides*)

a thin rectangular vase (scrupulously cleaned – gerberas are very susceptible to bacteria)

clear pot tape

a strong pair of sharp floristry scissors or secateurs

1 When creating a vase arrangement for a home or office, I will often use branches as the structure. To keep the twigs upright I first create a grid with the clear tape, as shown here. Then I place the *Mitsumata* in a linear pattern to create a good structure to arrange and hold the gerberas. Gerberas do not like deep water because of their hairy stems, so fill the vase to a depth of just 10cm (4 inches) or so, mixed with some flower food.

2 Place the gerberas one colour at a time throughout the design, taking care to decide the direction of the flower heads according to whether the arrangement is to be viewed as a front-facing piece or observed from all angles. Add all three varieties.

3 Finally, conceal the tape by placing the Spanish moss across the top of the vase. Allow some to trail down for a softer edge.

Thinking about colour

The most wonderful part of working with flowers is that you get to work with the most amazing range of colours. New varieties are constantly being presented and you have the chance to experiment with new shades each day. When working professionally with flowers, you find that colour is often the first decision a client will make, and colour defines the way you purchase and use flowers. There are the core palettes from which you can choose your flowers, to create a monochromatic or single-palette arrangement, or you can choose to mix palettes to create a fusion of colour.

THIS PAGE From late April to May, foxgloves grow wild in woods and I can enjoy their vibrant pink tones. I grow some cultivars in my garden and make the most of the limited supply of cut foxgloves when they are in season in May.
OPPOSITE These table posies include peonies, Purple Power roses, Babe spray roses, Carthamus 'Zanzibar', *Anethum graveolens* and orange *Gloriosa* 'Leonella'.

PREVIOUS PAGES A craze that began in Japan for decorative washi or masking tape gave me the idea for creating a pretty grid for a long, low glass vase. The tape is also functional; it holds the ranunculus, *Muscari*, *Viburnum opulus* and multi-headed *Narcissus* 'Soleil d'Or' in place. Electrical insulating tape is usually made in primary colours, and can be used inexpensively in the same way with a selection of boldly coloured tulips.

Core palettes

To understand how colours work well together you have to study some colour theory, in relation to a colour wheel. Harmonious colours are those that sit next to one another on the colour wheel, or very close to it. For example, red is near orange and pink and so that would be a harmonious colour scheme, balanced and easy on the eye. Complementary colours are opposite one another on the colour wheel. So green and red, blue and orange and purple and yellow are in this colour family. Mixing colours or contrasting colours is using colour to the maximum, and using one colour to make the other colour more pronounced. Any colour can be made to work with another colour, as it is all about balance and texture. The green from the foliage can be used to make the colour combination less dramatic or more zingy. Dark green glossy foliage absorbs some of the colour, whereas lime green accentuates colours and makes them brighter.

OPPOSITE What stunning colours: *Achillea* 'Moonshine', *Crocosmia* 'Lucificer', *Daucus carota*, *Hydrangea macrophylla* 'Blue Sky', *Helianthus annuus* 'Sunrich Lemon' and *Dahlia* 'Lemon Snow'.

The white palette

Top row from left: Paperwhite narcissus; *Euphorbia fulgens*; 'Kobe' phalaenopsis orchid; lily of the valley.
Bottom row from left: *Leucojum vernum* (spring snowflake); hydrangea; marguerite daisy; eucharis lily.

White, which strictly speaking is the absence of any colour, is the most popular hue in the plant world. It's the 'go-to' colour when we don't really know what colour to choose. Associated with purity, and the preferred choice for weddings, it is chic and sophisticated and always in style.

Top row from left: 'Siberia' lily; *Hydrangea arborescens* 'Annabelle'; *Helleborus niger*, *Gardenia jasminoides*.
Bottom row from left: Vendela rose; 'Ice Queen' gerbera; Margaret Merril rose; Akito roses and bouvardia.

THIS PAGE Pure and simple: a mass of white freesias and white lilac in a divine white-washed trug. These are pretty and practical items for younger bridesmaids to carry at weddings as they are easy to set down and pick up.
OPPOSITE Organic pottery vases display a selection of white daisies, dahlias and sweet peas. The mixed vases include molucella, dock, *Alchemilla mollis*, zinnias, Avalanche+ spray roses and seedheads from some dock weeds.

The pink palette

Top row from left: Pale pink sweet peas; *Prunus cerasifera* 'Nigra'; 'Bridal Kimsey' gerberas; 'Elbrus Pink' chrysanthemum.
Bottom row from left: *Camellia japonica* 'Peppermint'; 'Sonate' anthurium; 'Sarah Bernhardt' peony; 'Chessington Lilac' chrysanthemum.

Pink is my favourite colour and many pink flowers are on my most desirable list. The pink palette is very diverse, from palest shell to screaming fuchsia. Shy and light pinks or in-your-face shocking pinks give the floral designer a huge range of plant material through any season.

Top row from left: Zinnia; 'Onesta' dahlia; Gertrude Jekyll rose; 'Ville de Lion' clematis.
Bottom row from left: Ornamental kale *Brassica oleracea* 'Rose Crane'; 'Clooney' ranunculus; *Gloriosa rothschildiana*; 'Serena' gerbera.

THIS PAGE The muted tones of dusty pink with brown is one of my favourite combinations in mid-summer. 'Sarah Bernhardt' peonies are hand tied with brown Amnésia, pale pink Sweet Avalanche+ and pink Two Faces+ roses, poppy seedheads, photinia, *Alchemilla mollis* and *Anethum graveleons*.
OPPOSITE A more autumnal bouquet includes *Hydrangea arborescens* 'Annabelle', *Hydrangea macrophylla* 'Magical Coral', blackberries, jasmine, Titanic roses, pink veronica, *Viburnum opulus*, 'Diana's Memory' and 'Café au Lait' dahlias and cotinus.

The yellow palette

Top row from left: 'Ausoply' (Charlotte) rose; double peony tulips; yellow spider (Anastasia) chrysanthemum; *Narcissus* 'Grand Soleil d'Or'.
Bottom row from left: *Primula vulgaris* (primrose); Alexis rose; 'Lemon Ice' gerbera; *Helianthus annuus* (sunflower).

Certain flowers make yellow popular at different times of the year. In spring, it is the colour that excites us most after the dormant winter period. In autumn, sunflowers, heleniums, achillea and dill make it popular again. Mellow and creamy yellows are also popular choices now for flower growers.

Top row from left: 'Dante Yellow' chrysanthemum; *Gloriosa superba* 'Red Stripe'; 'Nettie' dahlia; Florida rose.
Bottom row from left: Crème de la Crème rose; 'Pauline Gold' ranunculus; Tara rose; 'Tom Pearce' chrysanthemum.

THIS PAGE The sharpness of this combination of *Helleborus argutifolius*, 'Dutch Master' daffodils, alder catkins, veronica, lysimachia, marguerite daisies and yellow ranunculus, with its glowing yellows and almost acidic greens, is wonderfully refreshing at the beginning of spring.

OPPOSITE A simple classic bouquet of creamy garden roses and a few sprigs of *Sanguisorba officinalis* 'Pink Tanna' looks good with most styles of wedding dresses.

The blue palette

Top row from left: *Muscari*; forget-me-nots; hydrangea and viburnum berries; aconitum.
Bottom row from left: Echinops; bluebell; 'Amazing Oslo' clematis; *Hydrangea macrophylla* 'Margarita'.

This palette offers a wide spectrum in the plant world, from deep blues through to the palest lilac. Essentially viewed as a masculine colour, blue is popular with clubs and businesses. I am most drawn to this palette in spring and early summer when some of my favourite blue flowers are prolific.

Top row from left: *Scabiosa caucasica;* aquilegia; eustoma (lisianthus); 'Kanchana Magic Blue' vanda orchid.
Bottom row from left: Veronica; *Scabiosa caucasica* 'Stäfa'; lavender; *Anemone coronaria* 'Mona Lisa Blue'.

RIGHT A ring of summer blues: individual posies are supported in test tube vases held on a metal stand. This allows thirsty flowers to stay fresh for longer. The flowers include *Hydrangea macrophylla* 'Margarita', *Centaurea cyanus* (cornflowers), forget-me-nots, *Astrantia* 'Roma', blue 'Amazing Oslo' clematis and purple 'Blue Pirouette' clematis, studded with small green apples.

The red to burgundy palette

Top row from left: *Hippeastrum* 'Tineke Verburg'; hips of Amazing Fantasy rose; 'Hunting Song' gladioli; 'Tiger Rag' chrysanthemums.
Bottom row from left: Canary tulip; Germini gerberas; 'Red Charm' peony; *Dianthus barbatus* (sweet William).

Red flowers are for romantic occasions and festive times – everybody recognizes the symbolism of the red rose. I also like to use red with other primary colours in the spring for bright and cheery arrangements. Burgundy makes a very dramatic effect, especially against peach or orange.

Top row from left: Anemone; 'Dark Rosy Reagan' chrysanthemum; *Hypericum* berries; *Sedum spectabile.*
Bottom row from left: Skimmia berries and red rose; autumn leaves of *Quercus rubra* (northern red oak); 'Red Charm' peony; 'Black Baccara' rose and red hibiscus.

THIS PAGE This simple moss wreath is wrapped with a rope of plump red hips threaded on reel wire to make a long, continuous necklace of hips. The spaces between are then studded with crab apples.

OPPOSITE Fiery autumn leaves are the colour inspiration for this hand-tied bouquet of hips, skimmia, carthamus, beech and roses, which is held in a vase within a fish bowl lined with chilli peppers.

The peach to brown palette

Top row from left: 'Avignon' tulips; Vendella and Primadonna roses; Marrakesh roses and astrantia; Trix, Tropical Amazone and Apricot roses, 'Real' gerberas, *Viburnum tinus* and *Skimmia japonica* 'Rubella' berries.
Bottom row from left: Anna rose; Amnésia rose; cymbidium orchids; skimmia berries, rose hips, willow stems and Combo rose.

This palette is diverse and rich. Peach was a little out of fashion in the last decade and pink took the centre stage, but now it is back and sand and gold colours are the new trend. Muddier and browner versions of orange are the most fashionable, as well as metallic shades such as copper, brass and gold.

Top row from left: Seedheads of *Echinacea pupurea*; peony, dahlia and hydrangea; Eldorado rose; *Zantedeschia* (calla lily).
Bottom row from left: 'Marrakesh' roses; 'Pauline Violet' ranunculus; pine cones; *Cosmos atrosanguineus* (chocolate cosmos).

THIS PAGE This summer arrangement is made up of grouped 'Coral Charm' peonies, Amalia, Marrakesh and Peppermint roses with purple astrantia, *Photinia* 'Red Robin' and viburnum berries.
OPPOSITE This wonderfully textural wreath, set on a base of a mossed ring, has an abundant autumnal mix of *Viburnum opulus* berries, apples, chestnuts, some very realistic fake mushrooms, lotus seedheads, alder catkins and berries from the *Solanum integrifolium* climber.

Seasonal palettes

Despite the wide palette of colours available to the flower enthusiast throughout the year, colour is still very seasonal. In the same way we are drawn to seasonal products for our food, we also want to see seasonal flowers. The international export trade has meant that you can get most flowers at any time, but there has been a reaction against that, and the current trend is to favour locally grown and seasonal blooms.

In early spring, after the dreary winter, we are drawn to fresh whites. As the seasons unfold we can enjoy all the pastel spring flowers and blossoms, and also the more vibrant primary colours. Mixed tulips in rich colours makes a very cheerful vase for the spring. The palette widens out from April, and between then until the Chelsea Flower Show at the end of May is my favourite time for seasonal flowers.

As the summer goes on you start to see a lot more seasonal blues, such as delphiniums, agapanthus, cornflowers, veronica and scabious. From June to August is the most plentiful time for the local cut-flower industry and the colour palette is at its most diverse. Towards the end of the summer, the yellows, oranges and browns start to predominate, and berries, grasses and seedheads herald the autumn. This is also a good time for purples, with delphiniums, hydrangea, larkspur, thistles and ornamental cabbages. Berries continue into winter, and red and white are the most important colours for the festive season, but green also takes the stage. We festoon our homes with greenery until nature's circle of renewal starts in the new year.

OPPOSITE Yellow is a key colour in spring, and *Narcissus* 'Grand Soleil d'Or' is one of the essential flowers.

The best spring pastels

1 *Narcissus* 'Avalanche'
Reliable and long-lasting as a cut flower, *Narcissus* are among my favourite flowers, and have been an enduring presence in my designs.
Other varieties: *Narcissus* 'Ice Follies'

2 *Prunus mume* (plum blossom)
Blossom is sold from February to April. If you buy the flowers in bud they usually last a week. I like branches arranged on their own in a tall vintage jug, or with pink tulips arranged at the base.
Other varieties: *Prunus* × *cistena*, *Prunus cerasifera* 'Nigra'

3 *Tulipa* 'Weber's Parrot'
This pale pink parrot tulip has been one of my favourites for 30 years.
Other varieties: 'Salmon Parrot', 'Super Parrot'

4 *Camellia* 'Chamaeleon'
There is something so perfect and appealing about the shape of the camellia flower.
Other varieties: *Camellia* × *williamsii*

5 *Primula vulgaris*
Dainty primroses are adored in the wild, and as some of the first flowers of spring.
Other varieties: *Primula sieboldii*, *Primula auricula*

6 *Ranunculus* 'Cappuccino'
Ranunculus is an enduring favourite flower for me and I love this variety.
Other varieties: 'Hanoi', 'Mistral Apricot', *Ranunculus asiaticus* 'Elegance Pastel Pink'

7 *Helleborus* x *ericsmithii* 'Winter Sunshine'
A real beauty of a hellebore, this variety is from Roger Harvey's nursery in Suffolk. A long-lasting plant in the garden, it makes a good cut flower too.
Other varieties: 'Christmas Glory', 'Harvington Single'

8 *Lathyrus* 'Pink pearl'
Fragrant and delicate, these flowers are among my top ten. They last better in water than foam.
Other varieties: 'Tickled Pink', 'Eleanore Udall'

9 *Hyacinthus orientalis* 'Fondant'
Long-lasting, very fragrant flowers, hyacinths are popular for posies and vases.
Other varieties: 'Anna Marie', 'Pink Pearl'

THIS PAGE The spray rose Olesya ('Intergoudia') is given a fragrant touch with early sweet peas and jasmine. A sharp touch of lime green, in the form of *Viburnum opulus* and *Thlaspi*, lightens the arrangement and the tiny spires of *Veronica* 'Caya' give movement.
OPPOSITE Sweet pea production starts for Valentine's Day, and this scented vase contains flowering mint, guelder roses, *Viburnum opulus*, *Myosotis sylvatica* (forget-me-nots), *Senecio cineraria* (dusty miller) and Bombastic spray roses.

The best spring brights

1 *Hyacinthus orientalis* **'Atlantic'**
Great cut flower but also good to use planted in arrangements and long-lasting designs.

2 *Hyacinthus orientalis* **'Woodstock'**
This is a deep almost beetroot shade, and the delicious heady aroma is another plus.

3 *Viburnum opulus*
Guelder roses are such a good spring green – it complements all colour schemes and makes designs zing.
Alternatives: Other good spring greens include *Helleborus* 'Double Green' and *Dianthus barbatus* 'Green Trick'

4 *Acacia dealbata*
Mimosa is such a pretty flower, with masses of scented yellow pom poms.
Other varieties: 'Mirandole', *Acacia baileyana* 'Purpurea', *Acacia floribunda*

5 *Narcissus*
So many gorgeous varieties to choose from. The two shown here are 'Carlton' and the orange-centred 'Pinza'.
Other varieties: 'Grand Soleil d'Or', 'Tahiti', 'Martinette'

6 *Ranunculus* **'Hot Pink'**
This gorgeous flower is on my market lists from February to April.
Other varieties: *Ranunculus asiaticus* 'Glamorous Pink', 'Amandine Bonbon'

7 *Tulipa* **'Queensland'**
The double dusty rose colour merges to a blush pink. It is paired here with another fringed variety, 'Huis ten Bosch', which has blossom pink edges merging to white.
Other varieties: 'Queen of Marvel' is deep pink and 'Blue Diamond' is purple

8 *Syringa vulgaris* **'Hugo Koster'**
Inspirational and nostalgic spring branches, some scented varieties.
Other varieties: 'Sensation' is lilac coloured, *S. x hyacinthiflora* 'Pocahontas' is purple

9 *Anemone coronaria*
Another cottage garden favourite that is popular with all. These jewel-coloured ones are 'Jerusalem Blue' and 'Marianne Orchid'.
Other varieties: 'Meron Bordeaux', 'Marianne Blue'

THIS PAGE The wonder of spring is the re-birth of nature and all the pleasure that brings to the flower lover and designer. This vibrant and scented basket includes *Narcissus*, hyacinths, lilac and grape hyacinths.

THIS PAGE This scented spring posy of lilac, guelder rose, daffodils, mimosa, freesia, ranunculus and tulips ('Negrita' and 'Madison Garden') is a tightly packed bundle of delight to me.

The best summer blues

**1 *Muscari armeniacum*
'Blue Spike'**
Delicate but delectable, everyone
delights at the sight of grape
hyacinths.
Other varieties: 'Blue Dream',
'Blue Eyes', 'Blue Star'

**2 *Nigella damascena*
'Powder Blue'**
Who can resist the delicate and
romantic love-in-a-mist? It works
well with sweet peas, *astrantia*
and *Alchemilla mollis*.

3 *Myosotis sylvatica*
Significant delicate flower whose
common name forget-me-not
makes it an emotional favourite.
Other varieties: *Myosotis
sylvatica* 'Victoria Blue',
Myosotis albiflora

**4 *Hydrangea macrophylla*
'Challenge Blue'**
Large mop heads make this a great
bloom for mixed arrangements or
massed on its own.
Other varieties: 'Blue Bonnet',
'Blue Tit'

**5 *Echinops bannaticus*
'Blue Globe'**
Greyish blue spiky globe that
makes an interesting flower in a
supporting role or on its own in an
architectural design.
Other varieties: 'Taplow Blue'
'Veitch's Blue'

**6 *Lavandula angustifolia*
'Hidcote'**
Lovely dark blue variety of lavender
that smells divine.
Other varieties: 'Munstead' is
another common variety, 'Alba'
is the white variety

7 *Veronica* 'Dark Martje'
Spiky dancing flower that looks
good in arrangements and hand-
tied bouquets as it adds movement.
Other varieties: 'Anna' is pink
and 'Caya' is white

8 *Scilla sibirica*
As a wild flower, the bluebell likes a
shady spot, but it is also cultivated
as a cut flower in the Netherlands.

**9 *Aconitum*
'Spark's Variety'**
Monkshood has spires of deepest
purple flowers, is available as a cut
flower throughout the year, but is a
late summer flower in the garden.
Beware, it is extremely poisonous.
Other varieties: *Aconitum
carmichaelli*, *Aconitum napellus*

OPPOSITE *Scabiosa caucasica* 'Lisa'
is studded with 'Hidcote' lavender and
edged with the felted grey leaves of
dusty miller, or *Senecio cineraria*.
THIS PAGE A wooden and metal urn
holds a formal arrangement of mid-
summer flowers. *Brachyglottis* 'Sunshine'
and *Alchemilla mollis* combine with
hydrangea, sweet pea, astilbe, nigella
and garden roses.

The best mixed summer colours

1 Paeonia 'Kansas'
Everybody adores peonies. Mostly we think of the white and the pale pink, but I love the fuchsia pink varieties too.
Other varieties: *Paeonia lactiflora* 'Karl Rosenfield', 'Barbara'

2 Hydrangea 'Rodeo Purple'
Hydrangeas offer so many gorgeous colours and shades.
Other varieties: 'Esmee Purple', 'Glowing Alps Purple'

3 Rosa Gertrude Jekyll
My own personal favourite garden rose flowers from June to September.
Other varieties: 'Princess Anne', 'Princess Michael of Kent'

4 Rosa 'Auspoly'
Previously known as Charlotte. Cream roses are the ultimate in sophistication.
Other varieties: Lichfield Angel, Ice Cream

5 Phlox 'Miss Fiona'
Gardeners have always loved phlox for their colour and scent, and for flower arrangements they are a great filler flower. They look frail but last well.
Other varieties: *Phlox paniculata* 'Bright Eyes', 'Aureole'

6 Papaver 'Apricot Parrot'
Poppies are available in winter from Italy and summer from the Netherlands. It's important to remember to singe the end of the stem when using them.
Other varieties: 'Patty's Plum', *Papaver orientale* 'Red Star'

7 Dahlia 'Purple Gem'
Dahlias are so in vogue for their colours and shapes.
Other varieties: 'Karma Sangria', 'Nashville'

8 Gloriosa superba 'Rothschildiana'
I love this honeysuckle-shaped bright flower, and the new colours are highly prized.
Other varieties: 'Leonella', 'Southern Wind'

9 Scabiosa caucasica 'Midsummer Sky'
Long cottage garden favourites, scabious are increasing their popularity as a cut flower.
Other varieties: 'Staefa', 'Lisa', 'Lavender Scoop'

OPPOSITE A bright hand-tied bouquet sits in a matching bag. Orange 'Souvenir D'Ete' dahlias, 'Barbados' spray roses, assorted alstromeria, *Erigeron speciosus* 'Pink Jewel', *Anethum graveolens* (green dill) and *Eucalyptus pulverulenta* 'Baby Blue' make an exciting display.

THIS PAGE Purple hydrangea 'Pink Jewel', calla lily, flowering mint, origanum, *Viburnum opulus* berries, pink Lady Bombastic spray roses, *Astrantia* 'Roma' and 'Purple Gem' dahlias create a richly vibrant mix.

The best autumn brights

1 *Malus domestica* 'Discovery'
Small apples and crab apples can be used as decorations. Branches are great in pedestals or large urns, and the small fruits look attractive in glass vases or woven into wreaths or garlands. 'Discovery' has a great texture and colour.
Other varieties: 'Cox', 'Gala', 'Braeburn'

2 *Dahlia* 'New Orange'
This dahlia dazzles among the kumquats. There are so many great shades and shapes of dahlia.
Other varieties: 'Karma Sangria', 'David Howard', 'Sylvia'

3 *Viburnum opulus* berries
The rich berries of the guelder rose are like clusters of redcurrants.
Alternatives: Other good berries are *Hypericum* 'Candy Flair', *Callicarpa bodinieri* var. *giraldii* 'Profusion'

4 *Triricum aestivum*
Having grown up in an arable farming area of the UK, I am always keen to use cereal crops in my arrangements, either fresh or dried. I had wheat at my own wedding as we married at harvest time.
Alternatives: *Hordeum vulgare* (barley), *Avena sativa* (oats)

5 *Chrysanthemum* 'Quinty'
Double spray chrysanthemums, such as this rich red variety, can be found really inexpensively at this time of year, so you can afford to buy them in large quantities.
Other varieties: 'Exopolis', 'Simple Red', 'Russet Gown'

6 *Aster* 'Cassandra'
Dainty daisies whose common name Michaelmas originated from the seasonal flowering in autumn. Available most of the year in a range of colours.
Other varieties: 'Caitlyn', 'Pink Pearl'

7 *Helianthus annuus* 'Sunrich Orange'
Great in hand-tied bouquets, or the larger varieties make great displays on their own.
Other varieties: 'Flame', 'Sunrich Gold'

8 *Auranticarpa rhombifolia*
These colourful orange berries resemble tiny pumpkins.
Alternatives: Other orange berries are *Ilex verticillata* 'Oudijk's Orange', *Hypericum x inodorum* 'Magical Pumpkin', 'Magical Fair' and 'Pumpkin' rose hips

9 *Chrysanthemum* 'Princess Armgard Red'
Bloom or standard chrysanthemums are very much in vogue again after decades out of the limelight.
Other varieties: 'Palador Dark', 'Tom Pearce'

OPPOSITE Autumn in a vase: Carluna roses , *Viburnum opulus* berries, *Daucus carota*, miniature sunflowers, elderberries, 'Black Lace' sambucus, *Sanguisorba officinalis*, *Anethum graveolens*, *Cotinus coggygria* 'Magical Green Fountain', *Chasmanthium latifolium* and *Leucothoe fontanesiana* 'Rainbow' make a rich mix.
THIS PAGE 'Golden Delicious' apples, echinacea seedheads, rosemary, sage, white nerines, a few stems of miscanthus grass and some hips create this very natural table centre. The glass bowl is filled with autumn leaves and wet floral foam to anchor the flowers. Twigs or kebab sticks can be used to anchor the heavier apples.

The best winter reds

1 *Hippeastrum* **'Tineke Verburg'**
Long lasting and impressive, I love to use amaryllis in all the shades of red and orange.
Other varieties: 'Bouquet', 'Nymph', 'Red Lion'

2 *Rosa* **Naomi** and *Rosa* **Black Baccara**
Red roses are a staple to use at any time of year, but are especially useful in winter.
Other varieties: Desire, Burgundy, Grand Prix

3 *Ilex aquifolium*
The common holly, known throughout the world as a symbol of the festive season.
Other varieties: 'Argentea Marginata', *Ilex × altaclerensis* 'Wilsonii'

4 *Rosa* **Sensational Fantasy**
These hips are available from late September to December. Perfect for texture and colour.
Other varieties: Magical Fantasy, Hip Hop Sunset

5 *Anthurium* **'Choco'**
A deep red and very long-lasting flower. Hugely underrated, it stays fresh for long stretches over the festive season.
Other varieties: 'Fire Red', 'Tropical'

6 *Hypericum* **'Coco Rico'**
A great medium-sized brown-berried hypericum.
Other varieties: 'Coco Grande', 'Magical Mocca'

7 *Dahlia* **'Arabian Night'**
One of my favourite deep red varieties.
Other varieties: 'Red Fox', 'Red Cap', 'Nescio'

8 *Rosa* **Passion**
A small neat-headed red rose.
Other varieties: Furiosa, Madam Red

9 *Anemone* **'Jerusalem'**
A superb winter flower and much loved.
Other varieties: 'Marianne Red', 'Deep Red', 'Monalisa Red'

RIGHT Every now and then a new flower appears on the scene and *Jatropha integerrima* 'Firecracker' is certainly unique. A tropical flower, it resembles coral and is a strong and long-lasting bloom. It is arranged here in a red lacquered boat with ivy, apple branches, viburnum berries, Cappuccino roses and a touch of cotinus.

THIS PAGE Dogwood is a must in winter, and *Cornus sanguinia* 'Midwinter' is one of the best varieties. The gradient of colour in the stems from orange, through yellow to red, is stunning. Here, it has been used to simple effect with amaryllis. The glass vase was lined with pomegranate slices to hide the stems and to reflect the rich-toned colours.

THIS PAGE This monumental suspended wreath is made from dried pomegranates glued onto a straw frame. For the mantelpiece decorations I used variegated foliages and a few thick pillar candles. It is amazing how long a simple foliage arrangement lasts. Ivy, holly, photinia and senecio look very festive with just a few wired ribbon bows.

The best winter whites

1   Heracleum sphondylium
Frost beautifies seedheads left in the garden, such as these umbels of hogweed, and winter makes you appreciate shapes found in nature.

2   Galanthus nivalis
The wild snowdrop is one of the most impressive of these bulb flowers, the first to break through the frosty earth after Christmas.

3   Hippeastrum 'Christmas Gift'
This gorgeous white amaryllis is great for lasting between Christmas Eve and New Year.
Other varieties: 'Challenger', 'Limona', 'Mont Blanc'

4   Helleborus niger 'White Magic'
Loved by all, the so-called 'Christmas rose' appears just before Christmas as a cut flower.
Other varieties: 'Christmas Star', *Helleborus* x *hybridus* 'White Lady'

5   Leucojum aestivum
Known as the summer snowflake, but it actually flowers in the spring. Looks like a giant snowdrop, and very dainty too.
Other varieties: *Leucojum vernum* flowers earlier, but it is not widely cultivated as a cut flower

6   Gardenia jasminoides
Grown for their attractive foliage and scented cream flowers, and used primarily for buttonholes and other wedding flowers.
Other varieties: *Gardenia jasminoides* 'Kleim's Hardy' is a very fragrant single form

7   Narcissus papyraceus
Paperwhites are a lovely scented flower that we all adore to have in our homes for the festive season and early spring.
Other varieties: 'Ziva', *Narcissus tazetta* 'Paperwhite', 'Erlicheer'

8   Galanthus elwesii
In recent years there has been a huge interest in snowdrops and galanthophiles are busy creating new varieties.
Other varieties: My personal favourite is the double variety *Galanthus nivalis* f. *pleniflorus* 'Flore Pleno'

9   Phalaenopsis 'Kobe'
Long-lasting cut flower for the winter months when we spend a lot of time indoors. Lasts longest as a plant, but will also keep three weeks or more in water.
Other varieties: 'Anthura Sofia', 'Sensation White'

OPPOSITE Shot glasses in a ring make a simple table centre when filled with snowdrops and sprigs of jasmine. Twisted decorative florist wire has been gently wound around the stems for added visual interest.
THIS PAGE To create a candle centrepiece, line a terracotta pot with foam. Add lichen-covered twigs, skimmia, hypericum, eucalyptus and *Viburnum tinus* berries and flowers and contorted willow, then finally some small-headed Akito roses.

Working with flowers

It is such a privilege to work with flowers and enjoy their beauty and charm each day. Although flowers have been cultivated since medieval times, it was only in the 20th century that flowers became a huge global business worth billions. They have become a commodity traded across the world on a massive scale; it is estimated that 60 per cent of the flowers traded in the world have travelled through one of the huge auctions in the Netherlands. Intensive farming around the clock has presented the flower lover with a huge range of flowers available in any season. Some flowers are so popular they become an all-year flower: there is no season and they are cropped and sent to market each week. Even bulb flowers like lilies can be tricked into production by climate and light controls. Most of the industry staples are post-harvest treated and can be chilled or even 'put to sleep' so they don't continue blooming and developing. There are ethical concerns about the intense production of flowers in Kenya and South America, and some of this controversy has driven the movement back for more sustainable, locally grown flowers.

THIS PAGE Calla lilies are stylish flowers. They look good in any environment and are easy to arrange. This one is *Zantedeschia aethiopica* 'Crowborough'.
OPPOSITE What a rich source we have to work with: echinops, scabious, hydrangeas, cornflowers, *Viburnum opulus*, roses and double eustoma wait to be made up into a wonderful bouquet.

Muse flowers

These flowers are the ones that inspire me to create a new design or a new colour scheme. Sometimes they are favourites from my childhood, such as tulips, peonies and roses. Ranunculus also hold a special place for me as they remind me of the marsh marigolds that I used to find as a child, and they inspired me to change my career from history teacher to florist. The muse flower can be the start of an arrangement or it can be the theme for an event. Often, seeing a flower in a garden setting can stimulate creativity. All the flowers in this section have so many varieties and colours to explore that they always appear in my designs. A visit to the huge Dutch auctions or the Royal FloraHolland trade show in Aalsmeer, will often lead to the discovery of a new muse flower. Whenever I travel to demonstrate or to teach, foreign flower markets are very inspiring. The San Francisco flower market is a great place to visit, and the Japanese flower markets display the produce of some very talented niche growers of sweet peas, ranunculus and gloriosia, and something new or rare and seasonal might catch my eye.

OPPOSITE The quintessential English rose Gertrude Jekyll is simply the best. I love the colour and the shape.

Ranunculus

These little round rosette-style flowers are available from late winter to May in the UK. They have been developed in Italy, Holland and Japan, and there are new varieties available each year. They come in all grades and a large assortment of colours. They are delicate and their petals can bruise easily, but they are perfect for bouquets, wedding work, table centres and displayed simply in vases.

THIS PAGE This very contemporary table centrepiece uses the heavy contrast of the diagonally cut cigar reeds *Cannomois virgata* against the very delicate cappuccino-specked pink ranunculus and balls of fluffy green *Viburnum opulus*.

OPPOSITE Posies of ranunculus edged with galax leaves are ready for two lucky bridesmaids to carry. Ranunculus can make a great alternative to roses for wedding flowers as they have greater longevity and hold their shape well.

THIS PAGE Miniature arrangements with just a few simple blooms really allow you to appreciate the beauty of the flowers. Here, an exquisite ranunculus is accompanied by grape hyacinths, *Viburnum opulus* and multi-headed *Narcissus* 'Soleil d'Or'.

OPPOSITE This fragrant posy has blue hyacinth and sprays of yellow mimosa mixed with *Viburnum opulus*, catkins and yellow clonal ranunculus.

Wired bridal bouquet

The best time to produce this bouquet would be in May, when the peony season will have begun and ranunculus are in full flush. Wired bridal bouquets often contain very soft plant material. With really delicate flowers, like ranunculus and sweet peas, we may also add a little damp cotton wool to the base of the stem when we wire the flowers, so there is still some moisture to keep the flower fresh. We then tape over the wire and the cotton wool with floral tape so it is not visible.

1

2   3

You will need

10 stems of 'Clooney' ranunculus

a bunch of pink jasmine

2 bunches of pink sweet peas

2 bunches of purple sweet peas

5 'Sarah Bernhardt' peonies

8 stems of astrantia

a pack of lilac skeletonized leaves

a selection of different-sized florists' wires

a roll of green floral tape

a roll of silver wire

a length of pink ribbon

a pearl-headed pin

a strong pair of sharp floristry scissors or secateurs

1 Remove all the flower heads from their stems and wire using the appropriate-sized florist wire. The larger heads should be wired internally by placing the wire into the stem and up into the flower head. With branches of flowers like the astrantia, you can place a thin silver wire through a branch and loop one length of the wire over the other and the stem three times. (This is called a double-leg mount.) Delicate stems of jasmine and sweet pea can be wired in the same way. Cover the wire with the green floral tape.

2 Start to place all the flowers into a nice round posy shape. Take care not to cross your wires and use a mirror so that you can see the shape you are creating. Be careful with your

bouquet and stand it up in a heavy jug when you need to put it down to avoid damaging the delicate flowers. Wire the skeletonized leaves with a double-leg mount and place them round the bouquet. Bind in one place with a roll of silver wire.

3 Bind down the stem with a ribbon slightly diagonally and then back up the other side and either secure with a pearl-headed pin pushed into the centre of the bouquet and/ or by tying on with a bow.

Roses

Roses are a much-loved flower throughout the world and grace all our important celebrations and ceremonies. The selection is enormous, and it is undoubtedly the most popular flower for weddings. Recently, garden-style roses and spray roses have been the most prized. At the luxury end of the market there are new developments to enjoy each year, and roses come in all grades, lengths and values.

OPPOSITE A large hand-tied posy of Anna roses – this would make the perfect bouquet to celebrate the arrival of a baby girl.
BELOW RIGHT Felted grey verbascum leaves are wrapped around glass votives tied with ribbon and topped with more Anna roses.

THIS PAGE When choosing the flowers for a dense arrangement, such as this classical topiary with fruits and vegetables, it is advisable to use some larger-headed flowers or foliage to help cover the expanse. Here, ornamental kales make the perfect filler. Camellia leaves and skimmia also form the base with Aqua and Avalanche+ roses predominating in the design. Pussy willow has been added along the contours of the design to give a more natural feel.

OPPOSITE A densely packed heart of pink Wham, Pearl Avalanche+ roses and spray roses, yellow Catalina spray roses and Caraluna garden roses, interspersed with the tropical vine *Diplocyclos palmatus*, rosemary leaves and feathery astilbe flowers.

Gloriosa

This stunning little flower was first discovered by ZW Baron de Rothschild while bird-watching in Africa at the beginning of the 20th century and brought back for the Royal Horticultural Society to exhibit. It makes a powerful impact as its common name, flame lily, suggests. The national flower of Zimbabwe, it is sold in several lengths and often transported in an air bag as it is so delicate. Small stems are great for table vases or centres, and long stems are ideal for hand-tied bouquets and vase arrangements. Now available in a range of colours, this flower always grabs attention.

OPPOSITE One of my all-time favourite inspirational flowers has to be *Gloriosa superba* 'Rothschildiana' – it is a fantastic colour and shape, and often acts as a starting point for flower arrangements. **BELOW** Here it is combined with Tenga-venga roses, miniature sunflowers and a touch of ivy berries for these candle holders. The leaf lining the glass vases is the variegated *Cordyline fruticosa* 'Red Edge', which is available all year round.

Tulips

THIS PAGE Long French peach tulips in single vases make a simple but effective mantelpiece design.

The main season for tulips is from winter through to May and they are universally popular. I think of them as a very meritocratic flower, they look just as good in a jug on your kitchen table as they do in a classical urn in a castle. I prefer them arranged en masse rather than mixed with other flowers, as they continue to grow in water and so will move higher than other flowers. The supermodel French or Californian tulips are longer stemmed, and look fabulous with blossom and spring twigs.

LEFT I used mossy twigs from leafless trees as well as some early-flowering prunus for this arrangement, with 'Rilona' amaryllis as the perfect colour to combine with the elegant heads of 'Menton' tulips.

OPPOSITE A huge glass column is filled with long branches of pussy willow and swirls of extra tall 'Menton' tulips.

Wrapped tulip bouquet

Perhaps the most sophisticated tulips are the white and pastel ones and the cream 'Winterberg' is one of my favourite off-whites. Tulips are the perfect shape and size for hand-tied bouquets, but remember they will continue to grow when you put them in water. Try to use them a little deeper in a mixed display and be prepared to re-arrange if you want to contain them neatly in the arrangement. I strip any lower foliage from the stem before I arrange them to make them easier to handle, and to allow more water to reach the flower head.

You will need

10 stems of *Tulipa* 'Winterberg'

10 stems of cream *Ranunculus asiaticus*

5 stems of cream *Hyacinthus orientalis* 'City of Haarlem'

7 stems of *Rosa* Alexis

5 stems of *Viburnum opulus* 'Roseum'

5 stems of *Skimmia japonica* 'Fructo Alba'

3 stems of berried *Hedera helix*

a roll of bind wire

a roll of cream netting

a roll of cellophane

a length of ribbon

a strong pair of sharp floristry scissors or secateurs

1 Carefully remove any foliage from the lower stems of all the flowers. Arrange your materials in groups and begin to make the spiral bouquet by taking one central flower and placing plant material slightly at an angle to the left of the first central flower. This may start at an angle of around 30° and as you get to the end of the bouquet may be more like 45°. Continue doing this with 3 other stems, then twist the bunch around in your hand, and then add another 5 stems to the left. Continue twisting the bouquet every 5 pieces of plant material so you are working on all sides. Remember to continue to use pieces of foliage throughout the bouquet to help create the structure and add interest to the bouquet.

2 When you have added all the plant material, tie with the bind wire at the point where you have been holding the bouquet. Cut a piece of thick cellophane and place it around the base of the stems to create a bag for water. Tie the cellophane securely and fill the bag with water.

3 Cut a length of netting to go around the bouquet and tie around the middle with a 3-looped bow.

Peonies

The peony season is never long enough, and these gorgeous flowers are both grand and simple. Peonies are suitable for any occasion and any location. They come in many different shades, with white peonies being very popular for summer weddings. About 200 varieties are grown as commercially cut flowers, with pale pink 'Sarah Bernhardt' peonies being the most readily available. Beware of buying peonies at the end of the season as they have often been held in chillers – they don't open well or bloom as you would expect.

Formal linear table centre

When peonies are fully blown they are immensely grand and over the top, and here they are the focal flower of this spectacular wedding table centre. Peonies are available in many shades in their short season. The most sought after in recent years has been the 'Coral Charm' peony. It is such an exquisite shade, and the colour transforms as it matures, which makes it even more remarkable and spectacular.

1 Soak the foam for ten minutes until the bubbles cease to rise in the water. Taking the camellia foliage in lengths of around 12cm (5 inches), work your way across the centre of the foam so that it is placed in all directions from the centre line.

2 Work down to the table edge and up to a height of around 10cm (4 inches) so that the foliage covers the whole block with no foam showing. Taking the flowery sprigs of the photinia, work across from end to end.

3 Then take the lilacs and, raising them slightly higher than the foliage, give the arrangement some life with these dancing blossoms.

4 Next add the roses, zig-zagging across the centre of the design and down to the table edge.

5 The ranunculus will need careful handling, so grip them close to the foam when you push the stem of these flowers into the foam. Spread the colour across the design.

6 Add the lime-green viburnum into any dark gaps and to trail over the edge of the foam and onto the table. Add the peonies into good focal spots so they can be enjoyed. Then take the tulips and carefully push them into any gaps, using the full length of their stems to fill out the ends and the sides of the arrangement.

You will need

3 bunches of camellia foliage
5 bunches of flowering photinia
3 bunches of seasonal purple tree lilac
10 stems of 'Maiden's Blush' lilac
40 Peach Avalanche+ roses
30 cream clonal ranunculus
30 *Viburnum opulus*
20 'Coral Charm' peonies
20 'Duchesse de Nemours' peonies
50 fringed 'Huis ten Bosch' tulips
1-m (39-inch) floral foam Raquette
a strong pair of sharp floristry scissors or secateurs

RIGHT With a base of shiny camellia leaves and flowering photinia, this sumptuous table centre includes 'Duchess de Nemours' peonies. The stars of the show, however, are the fully open 'Coral Charm' peonies.

Trend flowers

For 30 years I have been observing the trends and sometimes even influencing them through my books and writings. However, the internet completely altered the way flowers were viewed and made the identification of them so much easier. When I first started to write books in the early 1990s, it was almost impossible to find the names of some of the flowers we had bought and photographed! Now everything is easily found and labelled on wholesale sites or identified through banks of images. Even the growers themselves catalogue the flowers. In turn Pinterest and Instagram, in particular, have come to unite flower lovers all over the world, and made the platform for sharing information and trends so strong. Sometimes these trends have surprised me and sometimes they have endured longer than I would have expected. The growers are always quick to respond to these changes and the availability perpetuates the trend. More varieties are created and sent to markets, and the trend becomes more interesting and established.

OPPOSITE Daisies in all their forms have had a huge resurgence recently. These small marguerite daisies have such wonderful cushion centres of yellow. Their shaggy petals make you want to see if 'he loves you' or 'loves you not'.

Succulents and air plants

The trend for succulents and air plants originated in California, where they grow well and are always popular in the flower markets. Their renaissance is mainly due to Pinterest and international wedding blogs. They come in many forms and shapes and a range of interesting colours, too. One bonus of these sturdy rosette plants is that they are virtually indestructible. You can cut their root off and wire them into a wedding bouquet or an arrangement and then afterwards you can repot them and they'll put down roots again. They are perfect for recycling, which makes them bang on trend.

BELOW For these table centre arrangements, succulents are wired into the baskets to create a more sculptural effect. Astrantia, garden roses, sweet peas, *Alchemilla mollis*, mint and clematis are added to the centrepiece.
OPPOSITE This is a very textural combination of flowers and foliages in muted silvers and whites, but with a little acid green. The air plants are *Tillandsia xerographica* and the base foliage is *Brachyglottis* 'Sunshine' and *Alchemilla mollis*. The rose is the very square-edged and petally Dolomiti. The white gerbera is 'Pole Ice', one of the purest white gerberas, and the green mini gerbera is 'Kermit'. There are also a few stems of the 'Venice' phalaenopsis woven through the design.

Natural basket

Tillandsia is a genus of around 650 species of perennial evergreen flowering plants. Most species are epiphytes – they grow without soil while attached to other plants – hence their common name of air plants. They are not generally seen and therefore they have great novelty value. As they live without soil there are countless ways to use them in hanging designs and more contemporary arrangements. Here I've used them alongside succulents to line a basket.

You will need

15 *Tillandsia xerographica* (air plants)

10 stems of *Eucalyptus pulverulenta* 'Baby Blue'

10 succulent plants or stems of echeveria varieties

a handful of carpet moss

10 stems of *Astrantia major* var. *rosea*

10 stems of *Viburnum opulus* 'Roseum'

10 stems of 'Mona Lisa Deep Blue' anemones

10 Faith roses

10 Cool Water roses

10 *Eustoma* 'Kyoto Purple'

3 stems of vanda orchids

a sturdy basket

a plastic pot

a bundle of 1.00-mm (18-gauge) wires

a length of 5-cm (2-inch) chicken wire

a strong pair of sharp floristry scissors or secateurs

1

2

1 First you need to attach the succulents and air plants to the wires. For the air plants, push a wire through the stem horizontally. Then bring both ends down in the same direction as the stem and twist one wire over the stem three times to create a double-leg mount to attach to the basket. Wire the stems of eucalyptus in

the same way. Use the same method for the succulents; however, they will also need a wire up through the centre of the stem to anchor them, as they are heavier.

2 Attach the wired succulents and air plants around the sides of the basket, using the eucalyptus to fill any gaps. When the basket is completed, place a plastic container inside it. Next, scrunch up a length of chicken wire and push it into the container, making sure the wire is proud of the edge of the container and the basket. Secure the container in the basket with moss and fill with water mixed with flower food. Wire three succulents, two air plants and some eucalyptus into the chicken wire to establish your structure.

3 Start to add your flowers, using the softer flowers first. Small dainty flowers need to be added in groups to look balanced with the large flower heads.

4 To finish off, cut the three stems of vanda orchids into two or three sections so that you can place them in key positions around the design.

3

4

Daisies

Understated and associated with innocence, daisies are a pleasing shape designed to attract insects. Daisies come in many sizes and forms. My favourite wild daisies are ox-eye daisies and the nearest form available as a cut flower are *Leucanthemum* varieties. I like to mix these with grasses and dill. For that wild-flower look use smaller daisies such as *Tanecetum* daisies, a genus that includes feverfew. They have a lovely herb scent and look great displayed in jugs and jars. The Michaelmas daisy is a useful filler or works well massed alone. All daisies are reliable and last well as cut flowers.

LEFT A rustic stand is topped with a topiary wreath frame of ivy to provide a base for a daisy ring with its own bow. A touch of asparagus fern was added to lighten the foliage. The flower heads are all individually placed in small plastic phials of water to keep them alive. The bow was made from chicken wire and ivy trails, decorated with *Leucanthemum* x *superbum* 'Becky' and 'Bournier' Santini chrysanthemums.
OPPOSITE Hundreds of individual flower heads of the white daisy *Chrysanthemum* 'White Reagan' are massed on floral foam balls with a central candle. The bottom of the floral foam is sliced off before construction so that the balls sit securely without rolling. The massed balls are interspersed between silver candelabras adorned with daisy garlands that also snake along the table. A single flower sits on each napkin.

OPPOSITE Birch baskets hold *Leucanthemum* × *superbum* 'Becky' daisies and seedheads of *Ammi visnaga*. Loose stems of *Briza* nod above.

THIS PAGE A sweet basket of stephanandra, snowberry and white 'Star of Billion' astrantia, with fronds of the yellow dill *Anethum graveolens* and more *Leucanthemum* × *superbum* 'Becky' daisies. Dill, being another wild flower, is one of my favourite partners for daisies – it makes the yellow disc of the daisy centre pop with colour.

Daisy table centre

I love the way these simple flowers have been made to look both natural and elegant when arranged in a vegetative or growing style on this foam wreath ring. Nature is the most wonderful teacher! I imagine walking through a field of ox-eye daisies or along a roadside verge of cow parsley when I take up my scissors to create this type of arrangement.

1 Soak the ring in water with flower food. Taking one of the woody foliages, first work your way around the floral foam ring. You need to make sure that some of the foliage is parallel to the table so that the ring is hidden when placed on the table.

2 Build up the foliage using many different types to give it a really natural and wild feel. When working on a design like this you need to take a very holistic approach and be inspired by nature.

3 Start to add some of the softer foliages, such as the *Alchemilla mollis*, and begin to make the foliages taller, as if growing in the garden. Keep moving around the ring or turning it to view it from all angles.

4 Add the flowers, placing some in at right angles and parallel to the table and then working long stems upwards, as if they are growing towards the light.

5 Add the longer stems of scabious and daisies and, in the words of the famous British floral decorator Constance Spry, leave room for the butterflies!

You will need

a selection of summery foliages: *Panicum*, *Viburnum opulus*, herbs, hebe, *Alchemilla mollis*

20 *Zinnia* 'Lilliput White'

10 *Tanacetum parthenium*

20 *Nigella damascena* double white love-in-a-mist

20 *Nigella damascena* 'Green Magic' love-in-a-mist

20 white *Scabiosa caucasica* 'Anika'

20 *Leucanthemum* × *superbum* 'Wirral Supreme'

20 *Leucanthemum* × *superbum* 'Becky'

45-cm (18-inch) floral foam ring

a strong pair of sharp floristry scissors or secateurs

5

LEFT For this simple, natural napkin ring pale green flower heads of *Helleborus orientalis* are combined with *Viburnum tinus* berries and ivy trails.
OPPOSITE This collection of late spring beauties – pink bergenia flowers mixed with a selection of delicately speckled hellebores – is arranged in a loose natural way. This kind of simple 'just picked' look is romantic and very much the current vogue for weddings, for example.

Hellebores

These very photogenic flowers can be tricky to use in arrangements because most varieties have nodding heads. These look droopy when you place them into an arrangement, and I would definitely avoid using most hellebores in floral foam. The lime-green seedheads of *Helleborus foetidus* I might use in foam, but generally hellebores need to be in water. Some hellebore aficionados suggest searing the stems in hot water, but I think whatever you do the best vase life you can get is two or maybe three days. As such they are best suited to celebrations such as weddings to make the most of their short-lived charms. *Helleborus niger,* the white Christmas rose, has a more upright habit and is more reliable than some other varieties.

THIS PAGE Hellebores and fritillaria make an informal posy for a spring bride or bridesmaid.
OPPOSITE One of the first flowers of the year, *Helleborus x hybridus,* is contained in a rustic twig basket constructed from trimmed birch stem.

Flower-shop favourites

This section is all about the flowers that are the staples of the flower industry. This is in no way an exclusive list, but it includes some flowers that are available all the year round and some other long-standing favourites that may have a shorter season. In the main these flowers are long-lasting and strong and that is why they are so popular with both the retailer and the end user. Two things have made me think about these flowers recently; the first was when I was asked to do some consultancy on a super yacht and cruise liner. Both were procuring flowers from the Netherlands but using a purchase order list that was about 15 years out of date! However, there were surprising similarities in the list with today's top choices. The second occasion was visiting the Royal FloraHolland show at Aalsmeer and seeing all the new developments in lilies, alstroemeria, lisianthus, gerberas, gladioli, anthuriums and orchids, and thinking how different these flowers are to the dreamy Instagram feeds of the locally sourced, garden and wild flower lovers. However, these are the flowers that do the job, that last a long time and, being extremely versatile, can be adapted into all sorts of bouquets and arrangements.

OPPOSITE Standard carnations come in a huge array of pink colours and I love the ones that are the closest to purple. 'Farida' is almost the colour of beetroot. Massed together, standard carnations are very textural and I prefer to use them cut short in domed hand-tied bouquets.

Gerberas

These happy flowers come in an array of eye-catching and joyful colours. At one time you could only get the regular large size, but over the years some very passionate gerbera growers have produced smaller ones to suit hand-tied bouquets and now you can get many exclusive varieties. There is the double-flowered small Pomponi gerbera and the shaggy Pasta or Springs large-flowered varieties, which are the novelties at the moment. Gerberas have hairy stems and so they don't like to be placed in deep water as the stems can become waterlogged and soggy. They are very susceptible to bacteria, and so they benefit from having scrupulously clean containers and a drop of chlorine bleach is a good idea. Flower food is also essential for these versatile flowers.

THIS PAGE Individual Germini gerberas repeated in small tank vases make an inexpensive floral statement. These colourful daisies, which originated in Africa, are now grown in all the major flower-producing regions of the world, all year round.

THIS PAGE A clashing combination of bright pinks and oranges makes a striking table centre: small orange 'Mistique' and 'Malibu' Germini gerberas are mixed with orange marigolds, astrantia, berried ivy, skimmia and Amalia and Prima Donna roses.

THIS PAGE These 'birthday cake' arrangements trimmed with candles are very popular for adult birthday parties. Pale pink 'Gerrie Hoek' dahlias and 'Bridal Kimsey' gerberas, along with Luxuria! roses, are massed on a base of floral foam in a plastic tray. The container is edged with double-sided tape on which galax leaves are pressed, and secured with aluminium wire.

Gerbera table centre

For this long, low table centre I chose to use a selection in various colours of the new Pomponi Germinis from the Dutch specialist gerbera growers, Holstein. They are multi-petalled and come in individual shades, but often in mixed coloured boxes, which appeals to me. I decided to combine them with another relative newcomer to the flower scene – the equally vibrant *Jatropha integerrima* 'Firecracker'.

1 As always when working with gerberas, make sure the container is thoroughly cleaned with chlorine, and then fill with water.

2 First weave through the flax leaves to give the design movement and make the flower heads work together. The long leaves suit the linear nature of the design. Cut the *Jatropha* into small branches and add to the vase.

3 Finally, trim and add the gerbera flower heads to the design. Mix up the colours and try to contrast them against one another to make the combinations more punchy.

You will need

a few stems of variegated or green reeds: I used Phornium, the New Zealand flax

5 stems of *Jatropha integerrima* 'Firecracker'

a box of Pomponi Germinis or other small gerberas

a long, low container: this clever glass vase is perfect for the a dining table and is from www.chive.com

a strong pair of sharp floristry scissors or secateurs

Calla lilies

The botanical name for these flowers is *Zantedeschia*, which is a bit of a mouthful, hence they are often referred to as arum or calla lilies. They come in a range of colours, from white through to black, and they are prized by floral designers across the world, because they are long and structural and work well in high-end designer floristry and competition pieces. Make sure the stems are firm when you buy callas and change the water frequently: the stems become mushy if there is too much bacteria in the water. The best varieties of new callas are the ones in the Captain calla family. They have a sturdier stem and rounded, firmer flowers.

OPPOSITE The muted dusty rose-pink shades of *Zantedeschia* 'Aurora', cream Talea+ roses and pink *Astilbe* 'Erica' are great for lifting a bridal bouquet from the wedding gown and creating a subtle yet warm rosy glow.

BELOW 'Chianti' calla lilies and tropical *Diplocyclos palmatus* vine swirl around a ring of glass balls. If the flowers are to be reflected from below, choose only the most perfect specimens.

Lilies

Lilium come in a range of colours, sizes and grades. The new trend is for even longer and stronger super lilies, which are over a metre tall. The oriental lilies are strongly scented as well. The distinctive large star-shaped flower is great for using in large pedestals and installations. Getting a lily to look good for a special occasion is quite an art. It takes five days for a lily to open and some of the new super lilies take nearly seven or ten days to get going. If lilies are cold stored for too long they don't last well, so never buy them if the green foliage does not look fresh. Lilies look good in arches and ceremony decorations for weddings, and they also work well in flower walls, the current trend. Their scent can be overpowering in a confined space, so take care.

BELOW Oriental lilies have a gorgeous heady scent and their large flower heads, as seen in this variety 'Lucille', hold their own in grand arrangements.
OPPOSITE Another oriental variety – 'Medusa' – is combined with *Stephanandra*, *Cotinus coggygria* 'Royal Purple', *Paeonia lactifolium* 'Karl Rosenfield', trailing amaranthus, *Dahlia* 'Karma Choc' and the small heads of *Allium sphaerocephalon*.

Free-standing amphora

To create a really large arrangement it is best to choose flowers of many different shapes. Tall flowers give the arrangement height, while round flowers and star-shaped flowers like the lilies give the arrangement body. Around a third of the arrangement will be made up of foliage and to create a really natural effect try to use at least five varieties. Pick some that are bushy, some that are tall and some that are trailing.

1

1 Line the pot with a plastic bucket. Use some scrunched up chicken wire to enable the rim of the pot to sit flush with the amphora. Fill with water mixed with flower food.

2 Using a mixture of the foliages create the outline of the arrangement you wish to create. For a large freestanding arrangement the flowers should be one and a half times the height of the container.

3 For a round arrangement all the stems should radiate from a central point. Once you have a good base and structure with the foliage you can start to add the flowers, beginning with the prunus.

4 Use trailing foliages such as the ruscus, Solomon's seal and willow to trail down over the front of the pot.

5 Next, add all the woody stems such as the lilac and the viburnum and all the tall spires such as moluccella, antirrhinum, larkspur and delphinium.

6 Finally, add the star-shaped lilies throughout the arrangement at different heights and depths and then place the peonies to fill out any gaps.

2

You will need

10 tall branches of *Prunus* 'Sato-zakura'

5 long branches of rhododendron

10 stems of *Salix babylonica* (willow)

10 *Lillium* 'Sorbonne'

15 stems of *Paeonia* 'Red Charm'

10 stems of *Viburnum opulus* 'Roseum'

10 stems of flowering *Photina fraseri* 'Red Robin'

10 tall branches of *Sorbus aria* 'Majestica'

10 stems of *Antirrhinum majus* 'Potomac Rose'

5 white *Delphinium elatum* 'Snow Queen Arrow'

15 stems of *Delphinium consolida* 'Pink Perfection' (larkspur)

10 stems of long *Ruscus hypophyllium*

10 stems of *Syringa vulgaris* 'Dark Koster' (lilac)

8 stems of *Polygonatum* × *hybridum* (Solomon's seal)

10 stems of *Moluccella laevis*

a stand and amphora

a plastic bucket filled with chicken wire

a strong pair of sharp floristry scissors or secateurs

3

4

5

6

Anemones

I think of anemones as a nostalgic flower, and many people have a romantic view of them. They are a cottage garden flower that punch way above their weight. Recent production in the Netherlands and Italy has meant that the new hybrids last really well in water, up to ten days. They are thirsty drinkers, so make sure you top the container up frequently. Anemones are on trend at the moment, especially for weddings and Valentine's Day. They come in beautiful jewel colours as well as white. They don't last well in foam as they have hollow stems, and so I prefer to arrange them in water with chicken wire or tape as support for longevity and ease.

BELOW Bold *Anemone coronaria* is combined with 'Mona Lisa Blue', *Viburnum opulus* 'Roseum', Camellia japonica, *Hyacinthus orientalis* 'Annalisa', *Veronica* 'Dark Martje', lilac (*Syringa vulgaris* 'Dark Koster'), *Ranunculus ranobelle* 'Inra Wit', 'Negritta' tulips, *Brachyglottis* 'Sunshine' and ivy. Wands of pussy willow are very malleable in the spring when the sap is rising so are excellent for lining circular straight-sided bowls.

THIS PAGE White anemones, *Muscari, Viburnum opulus*, 'Blue Diamond' tulips, Blue Pacific roses, 'Weber's Parrot' tulips, 'Atlantic' hyacinths, cream ranunculus and a touch of birch catkins have been spiralled into a hand-tied bouquet and swathed in net.

Chrysanthemums

Love them or hate them, chrysanthemums are undeniably hard-working, relatively inexpensive and offer a huge selection. I like the Santini varieties, the small chrysanthemums first developed for use in hand-tied bouquets, with smaller heads grouped close together. I also like the daisy varieties, and will often use these in sculptural shapes, such as balls. The uniformity of the heads of spray chrysanthemums has meant that they have long been popular in massing, particularly in the traditional funeral flower trade. The big trend now is for the big blooms, both shaggy and spiky types, in an array of colours. These are often transported in netting or a bag as they are susceptible to shattering if knocked in transit.

LEFT Less is more when you put together a sculptural arrangement. To exaggerate height, you can bind chrysanthemum heads on long stems at successive intervals with twine. The only other component is a stem of orange rose hips.
OPPOSITE *Chrysanthemum* 'Princess Armgard Red' is a real beauty – perfect for minimalist displays.

Rustic bouquet in a decorated basket

As well as being stars in their own right when you select the correct variety, chrysanthemums are always good mixers. There are lots of red daisy-style chrysanthemums with green centres, and two examples are the Santini types 'Adora' and 'Marek'. Here, they are combined with a selection of other inexpensive flowers such as astrantia and ornamental kale, and with some large-headed hydrangeas. The resulting bouquet is reminiscent of a well-stocked late-summer garden border.

You will need

3 bunches of dried wheat

some moss

a selection of garden flowers: along with the chrysanthemums, I used *Astrantia* 'Roma', ivy berries, Fantasy rose hips, *Skimmia japonica*, *Echinacea purpurea*, autumnal hydrangeas, September daisy 'Lisette' asters and 'New Crane' kales

a sturdy, loosely woven round basket

a glass vase or container

several lengths of raffia

a length of bind wire

a strong pair of sharp floristry scissors or secateurs

1 I love to adapt my own containers to make my flower arrangements look more natural and sculptural. Small wire baskets are perfect for this. First, make about 24 bunches of 4 or 5 wheat flower heads tied with raffia. Place these around the basket by tying into place so all the ears of grain are about the same height and they look like they are growing naturally. When you have completed the container, line it with moss and place a glass container in the centre so you can fill it with water and flower food.

2 Now you are ready to make the hand-tied bouquet. Place all the plant material in groups of the same flower and strip the lower half of the stem by removing the leaves and stray branches.

3 Taking one central flower and a piece of foliage, place one piece to the left, and continue until you have placed 5 pieces into the arrangement. Then twist it in your hand and place another 5. Continue until you have added all the plant material.

4 At this point all the stems should be spiralled in the same direction and the top of the bouquet should be round and domed. The place where you have been holding the bunch is the binding point – secure at this position with the bind wire. (*Continued overleaf*)

4

5 Tie round the binding point with raffia as tightly as you can without damaging the stems.

6 Re-cut the stems with a diagonal cut then check the arrangement fits neatly into the container in the centre of the basket. Cut through the bind wire and give a little shake to release the bunch slightly within its raffia tie.

6

5

Carnations

Carnations have suffered a bit of bad press, mostly because of their ubiquity. Standard carnations are now back in fashion, however, and there is an astonishing selection of colours. There is also renewed enthusiasm for the old-style border *Dianthus*, such as 'Doris Pink' and the new Minitiara spray carnations, which look more like spindly versions of Sweet William. There is a renaissance in *Dianthus* growing, with lots of new varieties being introduced each year. Some flowers just appeal to the growers and hybridizers, and keep re-inventing themselves.

THIS PAGE A basket filled with carpet moss and topped with some old garden favourites, such as *Dianthus* 'Monica Wyatt', border spray carnations, chrysanthemums, Michaelmas daisies, feverfew, *Alchemillia mollis* and eustoma.

THIS PAGE A selection of old-fashioned pinks, known in Tudor times as gillyflowers. In *The Winter's Tale*, Polixenes urges Perdita 'Then make your garden rich in gillyvors.'

Orchids

This is a hugely diverse family. The best known is the Cymbidium, sold as a cut flower in mini or large versions and in supply much of the year except July and August, when scant production raises the price. The Paphiopedilum, or slipper orchid, is a great beauty, but its distinctive shape makes it less popular than the ubiquitous Phalenopsis, which is produced in many colours, grades and lengths. The Vanda family is known for its spectacular colours and the longevity of its blooms. Singapore orchids, such as dendrobiums, have declined in use as other types have become more available. All orchids tend to be pricey, so in the retail market plants are more popular – they are less expensive, last longer and are readily available.

OPPOSITE Chunky ornamental kales, Avalanche+ roses and white Cymbidium orchids are softened with the addition of lilac and ruscus. Jasmine and stephanotis make this a fabulously perfumed combination.

RIGHT Pure white vanda orchids form a classic teardrop bridal bouquet. Again, jasmine makes the perfect scented companion.

Anthuriums

Originally from the rain forests of Colombia, anthuriums are now a commonly grown cut flower staple all over the world. They last a staggering amount of time and some of the new varieties can last in water over six weeks. They are often overlooked because 'they don't do anything' – in other words, they look the same the day they come in until they start to turn slightly brown or black when they are dying. Their waxy appearance makes them look a little unnatural, and this also puts some people off, but in certain types of contract work and designer floristry they can be reliable and spectacular. Two things to bear in mind: they don't like cold temperatures and under 6°C they can turn black. Salt in skin also turns the spathes black, so avoid handling them.

BELOW A structure of kiwi vine provides a frame through which some flexi grass has been woven. 'Cognac' anthuriums follow the flow of the kiwi vine, resulting in a lovely light and well-balanced arrangement.

THIS PAGE Miniature pink anthuriums nestle among Beauty By Oger, Halloween and Aroma roses. The dark red skimmia and a few brown rudbeckia heads bring the brown of the base – glycerined oak leaves wired onto a sturdy twiggy basket – through the arrangement.

LEFT 'Sunrich Lemon' and 'Flame' sunflowers – 'Flame' has two-tone petals – combine with *Achillea* 'Moonshine', *Crocosmia* 'Lucificer', *Daucus carota*, *Hydrangea macrophylla* 'Blue Sky' and *Dahlia* 'Lemon Snow'. This design is called a standing bouquet: it rests on its own stems in shallow water.

OPPOSITE 'Sunrich Gold' sunflowers have lovely green centres. Here they are tied to create a tree for a modern twist on a design originally shown in my first book almost 25 years ago. The two-layer arrangement has been softened with *Anethum graveolens*, *Helenium* 'Kanaria' and some banana fabric to give a softer and more natural look.

Sunflowers

The name sunflower comes from the way the head of the flower turns to follow the sun while they are growing. They range in size from miniature ones to giant heads. There are single-flowering and double varieties, and as well as golden and yellow a wide range of brown and wine colours to choose from in the main growing season, which is summer and autumn. Sunflowers are heavy drinkers and are usually best purchased when open. Remove nearly all the foliage from the stem, retaining just one or two leaves at the top of the stem. This allows more water to reach the head and improves longevity. Cheery flowers, they are popular for bouquets, late summer and autumn weddings, outdoor parties and kitchen table jugs.

Garden favourites

Up until around 50 or 60 years ago, many people had a productive garden with space devoted to home-grown vegetables and some cut flowers. When I was first in the flower business, there were still lots of smaller suppliers who sent in a few boxes or buckets of seasonal flowers. But as the flower business began to get more serious in the late 1980s these dwindled. Then the supermarkets became interested and consumed 50 per cent of the market. Flowers became a very standard offer; the range you found in the supermarket was only a fraction of the supply available, and was dominated by year-round, mass-produced blooms. More recently, however, the trend for 'grow your own' vegetables has expanded to include cut flowers. Some florists started supplementing their supply from wholesale markets by growing their own, and some people made the lifestyle choice to start growing flowers to supply markets and shops locally. Flowers you recognize from your own garden found their way back into the flower shops again, especially during the summer months. As the demand for locally or home-grown flowers intensified, supermarkets started to support local growers, and that meant there was more product to send into wholesale markets. So in a roundabout way the supermarkets have been the unlikely saviours of the local cut-flower industry.

OPPOSITE Tiny ceramic flower pots hold miniature hand-tied posies of garden finds. Some 'weeds' have also been included, such as the forget-me-nots and the clover.

Sweet peas

These were the flowers I chose to use to represent my new flower shop. A flower I had grown from seed as a child, it represents the kind of flowers I want to sell: seasonal, scented, colourful and beloved. Commercial growers of sweet peas tend to pick varieties that have long stems and larger flower heads with the best longevity. Colour is also very relevant, but sometimes these properties mean that the scent is lost. The most fragrant sweet peas tend to be the older varieties, and these often have short stems. They are also short-lived: maybe three days if you are lucky.

LEFT Sweet peas are tricky to wire as the stems are so delicate, but they can make stunning hand-tied wedding bouquets for bridesmaids or flower girls, used massed in one colour or in mixed colours. Individual colours also mix well with other flowers for bridal bouquets.
OPPOSITE A gorgeous scented hoop of mixed fragrant English sweet peas and trailing pea vines.

THIS PAGE Hanging pots from my garden hold everlasting sweet pea *Lathyrus grandiflorus*, mixed with *Saponaria* and valerian.

Scented circle

Delicate multicoloured sweet peas are set off beautifully by their textured foliage background. You only need short stems for this design, so you can make the most of older varieties, which tend to be shorter but carry the best scent – home-grown sweet peas are ideal. Avoid using scented candles, which will distract from the distinctive perfume of the flowers themselves.

You will need

2 bunches of galax

2 bunches of *Brachyglottis* 'Sunshine' (senecio)

at least 50 stems of sweet peas

a 30cm (12inch) foam ring in a plastic tray

a pack of thin taper candles

a strong pair of sharp floristry scissors or secateurs

1

2

3

1 Soak the ring for five minutes in tepid water. If you have some flower food then place it into the bowl as well, as it will help feed the flowers and counteract any bacteria. Before adding any flowers, green up the ring with the foliage. I like to use plastic-backed wreath frames wherever possible and to edge the ring with large leaves. Some of the easiest to use are galax. I find these to be just the right size and also they have lovely tough stems, which are easier to insert into the foam.

2 After you have edged all round the ring, add the senecio at different angles, creating a lovely rounded effect.

3 Next add the sweet peas, working from one end of the ring to the other, taking care to put them in at different heights and depths around the frame. Sweet peas have very delicate stems and so it is vital that you hold your hand as near to the flower heads as possible and push them into the foam very carefully to avoid breaking their fragile stems. Finally, add the candles by pushing down firmly into the soaked foam.

Garden roses

As with sweet peas, fragrance has largely been bred out of commercially grown roses. There are one or two growers who are trying to redress this by only producing fragrant varieties, but these are really designed for the wedding trade as their life is short and they are expensive. David Austin grow some cut roses, but some of the production is in Kenya, to get the sun required to make roses bloom. There are also lots of German specialist garden rose producers and many of the Dutch firms, such as VIP, are returning to the old methods, creating beautiful open roses with scent. These roses are always going to be more expensive than your standard supermarket rose. If scent is important to you the best solution is to procure some locally or grow them yourself!

OPPOSITE Mixed garden roses are combined with flowering mint, *Alchemilla mollis*, pink hydrangea and lavender. The bowl is internally lined with petals from the garden – pink hydrangea and rose.
THIS PAGE These wild dog roses remind me of long hazy summer days in the country. Apart from their wonderful shape I adore this shade of very pale pink.

Garden rose urn

Garden roses are predominantly hybrid roses that are grown as ornamental plants and are one of the most popular and widely cultivated plants, particularly in temperate climates. Constance Spry was an avid rose fan and spent years cultivating antique roses. When the now famous English rose breeder David Austin named his first rose in 1963, three years after her death, he proudly named it Constance Spry. Since then the Austin family has introduced nearly 200 new varieties. Many of these garden roses are grown and developed for cut flowers.

You will need

10 stems of *Alchemilla mollis*

10 stems of *Mentha longifolia* (silver mint)

10 stems of *Phytolacca americana* (pokeweed)

5 stems of *Borago officinalis* (borage)

10 stems of *Sanguisorba officinalis*

10 stems of *Monarda didyma* 'Pink Lace'

10 stems of *Daucus carota*

a bunch of *Chasmanthium latifolium*

5 Bubblegum roses

5 London Eye roses

5 Constance Spry roses

5 Caraluna roses

5 Romantic roses

5 Wedding bells roses

5 Alberic Barber cream roses

5 Awakening pink roses

a vintage low vase

a roll of clear tape

a strong pair of sharp floristry scissors or secateurs

1 First tape across the top of your container so you create a grid to hold the foliage in. Then fill up the vase with water mixed with flower food.

2 Taking the *Alchemilla mollis* first, create a good overall structure. Then add the mint taking care to make the stems radiate from the centre and not to be too upright, as this will not achieve a natural shape.

3 Start with the more hardy and firm flowers first, and create a structure of different head shapes. Move the vase around so you are working on all sides, and save some of the naturally drooping flowers for the sides. Dangle the pokeweed over the edge of the vase and use the floppy habit of the plant to give you some trails. Do the same with the borage, *Sanguisorba* and the grass. Always work with the shape of your plant material. Continue until you have achieved a good shape and the overall structure is ready to display the roses.

4 Finally, add the roses, mixing the colour throughout the arrangement. Top up the vase to the top as there is lot of plant material and it will need lots of water.

THIS PAGE You can also see this
Fulham Pottery Constance Spry vase on
page 28. For this arrangement I've used
a mix of garden roses and garden herbs
that Constance would have recognized.

Dahlias

From an unimpressive tuber a spectacular, prolific plant emerges! So what makes dahlias so impressive? Well it has to do with the fact that most plants only have two sets of chromosomes, while dahlias have eight. The hybridizers have gone to work to produce an astonishing variety of dahlias in all colours, shapes and sizes. Like chrysanthemums they are subject to shattering, so the fancier varieties don't travel well. The Karma range was developed for the cut-flower industry, and these have sturdier stems and last well. 'Karma Sangria' is my personal favourite.

LEFT A bridesmaid's bouquet of deep red peonies, eupatorium, nigella seed heads, dusty pink echinacea daisies and the sculptural flower heads of pale pink 'Wizard of Oz' dahlias.

OPPOSITE 'Café Au Lait' dahlias have been wowing the Instagram crowd for some time, and here it is hand-tied with Lady Bombastic Spray roses, *Thlaspi perfoliatum* 'Green Bell', *Senecio cineraria*, *Chasmanthium latifolium*, scented sweet peas (*Lathyrus odoratus*), cotinus and the scented herb *Origanum laevigatum* 'Purple Charm'. The lovely berried trails are pokeweed (*Phytolacca* 'Carbouzijn').

THIS PAGE A vibrant mixture of English dahlias in different sizes and shades is set off by a few sprigs of delicate dill umbels, or *Anethum graveolens*. They are arranged in one of my favourite vases. It is designed by two wonderful Parisian designers Tse & Tse Associates. This April vase is made from articulated steel; you can move it around into interesting shapes. It works with all flowers, so it is the vase equivalent of the Little Black Dress!

Delphiniums

Another quintessential summer flower, delphiniums come in several different sizes and grades. The long hybrid varieties are really flowers for grand occasions and for large decorative pieces. However, the smaller delphiniums are perfect for jugs and vases. The individual florets can also be wired into headdresses and wired bouquets. When you grow them in your garden it is vital to stake them to protect the stem, so look out for varieties with good sturdy stems.

THIS PAGE This harmonious vase combines seasonal flowers in greens, pinks and lilac, and includes a good mix of shapes such as the tall delphiniums, the round 'Shamrock' chrysanthemums and peony tulips, with lilac and guelder rose to fill. Light tendrils and buds of eustoma lighten the outline while the Solomon's seal creates a soft edge between arrangement and vase.
OPPOSITE In mid-summer there are lots of wonderful flowers on the market that are over 1m (3 feet) high. Here we had 1.2-m (4-foot) white delphinium and white eremurus at 1.5m (5 feet) – perfect for grand statement pedestal designs like this one.

THIS PAGE During the summer months I often find that I am drawn towards using glass in many of my designs, perhaps because of the higher light levels. This glass urn is filled with a bursting bouquet of delphiniums mixed with molucella, hydrangea, dahlias, peonies, trailing amaranthus, leycesteria, *Miscanthus* 'Rotfeder', astilbe, antirrhinums, *Alchemilla mollis*, poppy seedheads, *Pennisetum* and *Panicum* 'Warrior'.

Large-scale pedestal

These wonderful pedestals use lots of foliage and long branches and stems to make them look very natural. I adore the sharpness of the lime-green viburnum against the flower colours, and if I can sneak some scented flowers into an arrangement, such as lilac and stocks, I am in heaven. Don't forget to include some arched or trailing flowers. In spring and summer we have long and plentiful plant material and I often arrange in water so all the soft plant material can drink freely.

You will need

10 stems of magnolia branches

5 stems of long olive branches

15 stems of *Prunus cerasifera* 'Nigra'

110 each of 'Maiden's Blush' and 'Hugo Koster' lilac

10 *Viburnum opulus* 'Roseum'

10 each of 'Blue Skies' and Candle Lavender Group delphiniums

20 *Matthiola incana* 'Figora Light Rose' (stocks)

10 stems of *Hedera helix* (ivy trails)

10 stems of *Polygonatum multiflorum* (Solomon's seal)

20 Cool Water roses

10 'Robina' lilies

bucket set in a large urn with moss

a strong pair of sharp floristry scissors or secateurs

1

1 Secure the bucket into the container with moss so the edge is proud of the urn. Add water mixed with flower food.

2 Establish a frame for the flowers using branches of magnolia.

2

3

4

3 When you have a good structure you can begin to add the foliage. You should aim to make the arrangement at least one and a half times as high as the urn to create a visually pleasing effect. Next add the longer stems and the fuller flowers of the lilac and viburnum.

4 Add the tall spires of delphinium and stocks throughout the arrangement. Use the ivy and Solomon's seal to trail over the edge of the urn – this creates a natural feel.

5 Finally add the roses and the lilies in any gaps to create a massed flower effect.

5

OPPOSITE Arching stems of 'Delphi's Secret',
'Alis Duyvenstein' and 'Blue Star' delphiniums
combine with star-shaped 'Helvetia' Oriental lilies,
the round heads of *Hydrangea macrophylla* 'Rodea
Paars Classic' and 'Verena Classic' and generous
swathes of forsythia, stephandra and cotinus foliage
in this grand pedestal arrangement.
THIS PAGE A more informal feel is achieved with
a simple collar of hydrangea flowers and foliage
surrounding a vase of 'Delphi's Secret' delphiniums.

Lavender

I love to use fresh lavender, although the season is usually very short. It is best to buy lavender when it is fully developed, as it does not open further in water. Make sure it was cut during a dry patch and look for any mould. If it has been kept or cold-stored it tends to drop, so give it a quick shake before buying to check if that's the case. I prefer French and Italian lavender varieties, which are often a deeper blue than the English ones, but all varieties vary in shade and scent. Lavender has so many uses in floristry. When dried it looks very similar as when fresh, and works just as well.

LEFT Fresh lavender has been bunched and wired into a swag with wired fennel bulbs to create a lovely natural garden feel. Green and white hydrangea and blowsy garden roses are grouped on a base of *Viburnum tinus* berries.

OPPOSITE This lavender basket is always in popular demand for June weddings. The small bunches of lavender are tied to the basket with raffia and the interior is packed with moss. A plastic bowl filled with floral foam is added to the top and filled with scented mint, blackberries, *Alchemilla mollis* and masses of garden roses. This organic style works surprisingly well in modern interiors as well as rustic settings.

Lavender-trimmed basket

From June to late August there is a good supply of fresh lavender, and until it starts to drop it makes a wonderful decoration for bunching. This is a technique traditionally used for garlands, and many woodcarvings that date back to the Elizabethan period depict early examples. Bunches can also be tied onto a metal frame, as on this basket, or fixed onto plastic containers using double-sided tape. This requires quite a lot of time, and more lavender than you imagine!

You will need

5 bunches of lavender

20 stems of *Alchemilla mollis*

20 stems of flowering mint

5 stems of *Eryngium* 'Sirius Questar'

20 stems of garden roses

15 stems of *Leucanthemum ×
superbum* 'Wirral Supreme'

20 stems of *Scabiosa caucasica* 'Stäfa'

a few stems of clematis

a few sweet peas

a sturdy wire basket

a block of floral foam

a roll of ribbon or raffia

a strong pair of sharp floristry
scissors or secateurs

1

1 Gather your materials. I used a wirework basket, but you can also use a wicker one, provided it has an open weave so you can tie in the lavender stems. Divide your lavender into neat bunches. Trim some of the bunches so the flowers rise above the top of the basket. Tie in place with ribbon or raffia. Cut other bunches and place them onto the basket at different heights.

2 Continue until the whole basket is complete. Follow the shape of your chosen container – this one curves up to the handles – so that it looks well covered and has a lush effect.

2

3

4

3 Place a block of foam in the centre of the basket. You may need more than one, depending on the size of your basket, as you must make sure your block is as high as the top of the lavender to create the effect of a full basket.

4 Add the sprigs of *Alchemilla mollis* and then the flowering mint. Place every stem as if it is coming from the same central point of the arrangement. This gives a natural feel to the flowers.

5 Add the *Eryngium* – at this point you should not be able to see any of the green flower foam.

5

6

7

6 Add the roses next, trimming the ends of the stems before you push them carefully into the foam.

7 Finally, add all the remaining flowers, leaving those with weaker stems to the end. You will need to place your hand close to the foam and push in the stems very carefully.

Scabious

The blue scabious *Scabiosa caucasica* 'Stäfa' is the most common and well known. 'Midsummer' is a true blue variety, whereas 'Lisa' has a more lilac tint. There are also a few white varieties. Then there is the round seedhead of *Scabiosa stellata*, which is useful in summer bouquets and arrangements and even seems to find its way into buttonholes. The pincushion scabious, which looks more like the wild scabious, is the scabious of the moment. Growers in Israel have taken this one to their heart and are now producing colours that are known as the Scoop series. Popular with the new wild-flower design style, these are available from spring to late summer. They have narrow spindly stems which belie the fact that they can last ten days and are really quite strong.

BELOW A low silver and glass trough is filled with four individual posies of scabious, dill, echinops, cornflower, ivy berries and that indispensable summer filler plant, *Alchemilla mollis*.

OPPOSITE From above this wreath forms a tight circle, and its shape can be appreciated. The soft fluffy green flower heads of *Lagurus* grass, with their sword-like leaves poking through, form a counterpoint to the densely massed flowers. I chose a selection of high summer blooms, including scabious, sweet peas, veronica, roses, astrantia and thistles.

Scoop scabious pail

You will need

20 *Scabiosa caucasica* 'Lisa'

10 Picasso scabious

10 Candy Scoop scabious

10 Marshmallow Scoop scabious

20 Blackberry Scoop scabious

20 Lavender Scoop scabious

10 Cherry Vanilla Scoop scabious

a zinc pail

a length of 10-cm (2-inch) chicken wire

a strong pair of sharp floristry scissors or secateurs

The Scoop series was developed by a biotechnology company in Israel called Danzinger Innovations Ltd. They work on providing a reliable cut flower and have developed seven colours of the Scoop scabious for other growers to produce. Blackberry is the darkest and the palest is the white Vanilla. Candy, Marshmallow and Raspberry are shades of pink and Cherry Vanilla is aubergine coloured. The one that looks most like its wild family cousin is Lavender Scoop. Picasso is another good dark scabious.

1 Scrunch up a length of chicken wire and place it in the zinc bucket so it holds well and is firm. Add water mixed with flower food. Taking one colour first, arrange the scabious around the zinc bucket. All the stems should radiate from the central point and feel natural.

2 Continue with other colours. Keep turning the bucket as you go so you are working on all sides and the flowers all radiate from the same central point.

3 When you have finished adding the flowers, top up with water and flower food, as you have lots of thirsty stems that will quickly drink the water. Keep the water topped up and add more flower food every two days.

OPPOSITE This delightful posy with flowers of concentric circles is a modern take on a Victorian posy, sometimes referred to as 'Biedermeier' designs. A structural ring of fresh contorted willow holds an Alexis rose, *Muscari botryoides* 'Album', *Narcissus tazetta* 'Avalanche', 'Winterberg' tulips and *Fritillaria meleagris*.

RIGHT A sense of energy bursting through is suggested in this tight mass of plump buds and unfurling flowers. A posy of double peony tulips, scented *Mahonia Aquifolium*, ranunculus, yellow *Narcissus*, 'Dick Wilden' and cream *Narcissus* 'Geranium' with an orange centre, sits in a grey woven basket.

Narcissus

Always a meritocratic flower, *Narcissus* are easy to grow, readily available and inexpensive. There are lots of varieties sold both as cut flowers and as potted bulbs for flower arrangements and installations. The larger yellow variety is more commonly known as the daffodil, and is often not scented whereas the paler, smaller-headed varieties, which are scented, are often referred to as *Narcissus*. Various white varieties are commonly called 'paperwhite'. Some of my favourites are 'Avalanche', 'Ice Follies', 'Erlicheer', 'Geranium', 'Soleil D'O'r' and 'Dick Wilden', with a double trumpet.

Hydrangeas

These popular flowers are so useful in every type of design. Used singly, collected together or mixed with other flowers, they are a really hard-working bloom. If they do flag you can revive them totally in a bucket of water. I often use my bath at home, but at work we re-cut the stems and re-hydrate them in large bins. The tip for getting the best hydrangeas is to buy them with brown stems rather than green stems, as that indicates new growth rather than old growth. Surprisingly, Colombian hydrangeas, which travel so far, can be long lasting and reliable, possibly due to post-harvest chemical treatment.

LEFT This bridesmaid's hoop is simply bound with ivy and then covered with clematis and bunches of brodiaea and cornflowers. Wired heads of hydrangea are added through the ring.
OPPOSITE Pots lined with white heather are filled with multicoloured hydrangea heads, pistachio foliage, snowberry and white Avalanche+ roses.

OPPOSITE An asymmetrical arrangement was inspired by the shape of this branch of purple sloes – this plant can be spiky but it works well in a vase and holds its fruits. It is simply adorned with five huge heads of *Hydrangea macrophylla* 'Bela'.

THIS PAGE This tall thin vase arrangement has physical balance: the weight of the fritillarias is evenly distributed to make the vase stable. The willow gives more visual balance to the overall look and the collar of lilac hydrangea gives stability both in real terms and also visually.

Stems and foliage

The British tradition for floral design has always been in love with the use of foliage and seasonal branches. For a long time American floral design was obsessed with an all-flower look and used scant foliage, but now it has embraced a wilder look. Evergreen foliages and some greenery that is grown solely for the flower industry can be too uniform and stiff, and so I prefer to use seasonal foliages in all my designs. Depending on what I am aiming to create, I always try to use three different types of foliage to give the design a natural feel. There has been a huge change in the assortment and the availability of branches and flowers in the last 30 years. When I first started in floristry, it was very common for retail florists to only use cypress in arrangements. It was cheap, and the thinking was that people would prefer to spend money on flowers than on greenery. But in wedding work and for decorations, and also among flower arrangers, the use of foliage was always paramount to create the desired effect and provide structure and shape. Towards the end of the year, when we are decorating our homes for Christmas, the use of branches and foliages intensifies, and the ratio of flowers to greenery changes considerably. Evergreens, berries and seedheads that have been dried and sometimes painted, start to take centre stage in our work and designs.

OPPOSITE Pussy willow is the common name given to *Salix caprea*, which is a popular spring shrub. It is a plant that has a special place in the hearts and minds of nature lovers all over the world.

Bare stems and twigs

In the autumn when the sap falls and leaves drop, I am much more conscious of the bare stems in nature. From October through to March when the sap starts to rise again, I am drawn to use branches in our work. It might be contorted willow or hazel, which gives structure and height. I might even use large pieces to support test tubes or small vases, which I then fill with flowers. This creates a larger installation without using too much plant material. The branches can always be stored and used again, or even spray-painted for a different look.

LEFT Long stems of *Cymbidium* 'Rum Jungle' are given a suitably sculptural framework with these red-tinged stems of twisted willow. In a glass vase the whole of the stems can be appreciated.
OPPOSITE There are many different species of *Betula* and the catkins differ. This is *Betula utilis* var. *jacquemontii*. At Easter I usually make a large vase of twigs and decorate them with blown and artificial eggs, following the German tradition of the *Osterbaum*.

OPPOSITE The combination of blossom and serrated-edge tulips is as close as you get to origami in the flower world. It looks as though someone has cut these out of fine tissue paper; they are so delicate and perfect.

RIGHT So often in the spring garden there are reminders of the simple beauty of a single type of flower. Here a few branches of early pear blossom are such an interesting colour and shape they need no accompaniment.

Blossom branches

Blossom is one of the most revered flowers in the world, internationally recognized as a symbol of renewal and so uplifting. Blossom is sold from February to April, usually when the flower is in bud and it should last for about a week. The first blossom to appear in Europe comes from the San Remo growers on the Italian Riviera, and then the more local English blossoms are sent into the flower markets. We start with the blackthorn or sloe (*Prunus spinosa*) with its mass of white blossom. Yoshino cherry (*Prunus* x *yedoensis*) blossoms in late March and early April, in white or pale pink and has a delicate fragrance. The wild hawthorn blossom in pink or white is one of the latest.

Grasses

There are grasses around throughout the year, but the main season comes in the summer and autumn. *Panicum virgatum*, or fountain grass, is one of my favourites for summer bunches and table centres. Later millet grass, *Setaria italica*, in green and burgundy, gives a lovely droop to table designs or hand-tied bouquets. The new fashionable grass is the quaking grass, *Chasmanthium*, whose nodding heads give a little movement to any design. Sometimes it is available in very tall lengths and so is useful for large displays as well as miniature ones. The best all-year-round grasses are bear grass, lily grass, *Typha latifolia*, China grass, the variegated *Liriope muscari* or the green *Liriope gigantea, Ficinia fascicularis* – called flexigrass oddly, as it is erect – and steel grass, or *Xanthorrhoea australis*, which is strong and straight.

LEFT AND OPPOSITE I have always enjoyed tying flowers together at the base of their heads to make 'living topiary'. Here, bunches of the foxtail millet *Setaria italica* 'Tomer' have been bound together and placed in a blue glass vase in water. I added a little moss to the sides of the bunch to keep it upright.

Umbels

I adore the umbel shape. I guess it is the frothy cow parsley that got me into the shape as a child. In my mature years I think I love the cow parsley season more than any other time of the year. The umbrella shapes of the celery family, such as wild dill and parsley, look good until autumn and then some of them dry well. Near the old Spitalfield flower market on the banks of the River Lee in London there are still some giant hogweed. It is dangerously toxic, so you are no longer allowed to pick it or transport it, to avoid the spread of the seed, but I do remember some very spectacular displays with this giant umbel back when I started my flower journey. *Anethum graveolens* and *Daucus carota* are my favourites today, but I love *Ammi* too.

THIS PAGE *Ammi majus* and *A. visnaga* are the commercial equivalents of cow parsley, although they both last much better. *A. visnaga,* shown here, has perfect heads of little florets making up the delicate umbel.

OVERLEAF *Anethum graveolens* is one of my top umbels. I love the way it gives movement and adds to the colour!

THIS PAGE My mother's old biscuit barrel holds *Anethum graveolens*, 'Lemon Ice' dahlias, miniature sunflowers, *Daucus carota*, poppy seedheads, achillea and feverfew (*Tanacetum parthenium* 'Single Vegmo').

LEFT Lengths of clematis vine are twisted into a ring and wired into place as a basis for this harvest wreath. Bunches of assorted coloured peppers and differently coloured dried maize, or corn cobs, are then wired into the wreath, with raffia adding the final touches.

OPPOSITE For these stark and sculptural arrangements, trimmed stems of *Polygonum persicaria* are paired with green allium seedheads.

Seedheads

I am drawn to seedheads in the autumn and also in the winter as there are so many varieties to choose from. Fresh green seedheads, from poppies and lotus flowers, give a textural feel to arrangements, and in the winter when they are dried and painted they add some sparkle. In recent years seedheads from the *Allium* family have become very popular, despite the fragrance. From May to September different variations of the family are available and because they are so structural they are very arresting and elegant. The shaggy *Allium schubertii* is like a firework. Recently they appeared dipped in gold for the first time and now they are my favourite seedhead for the festive season!

Berried stems

When I first came into the flower business, berries were much more seasonal than they are today. *Hypericum* was only available in the autumn and in a few colours, but now there are 50 varieties in all colours, available all the year. Rose hips have exploded onto the market, too, with a few varieties now in wide-scale production and being sent into the auctions at lengths from 20cm to 1m (8 to 40 inches) or more. *Viburnum* berries in red and black are available for a good part of the autumn and winter. Texture became part of accepted good floral design and the growers took up the gauntlet. Favourites include snowberries, blackberries and metallic sloe berries (*Prunus spinosa*).

ABOVE Groups of rose hips, *Viburnum tinus* berries and astrantia have been arranged with Pepita spray roses in individual tumblers. Black cordyline leaves are tied around the tumblers with ribbon and lace to give a vintage feel.
OPPOSITE This uncomplicated vase of contorted willow, hips and apples will be long-lasting – if not kept too near the fire for long!

Trailing ivy

Out of all trailing foliages I use in my work, my favourite is ivy. I adore the way it graduates to the smaller leaves, and how the dark green leaves have veins. I know it is a beast in the garden if left to its own devices, but nothing gives a wild droop like a handful of green ivy. I am not so keen on the variegated form, as it is interferes with colour combinations, but the dark green tendrils always give movement to an arrangement. Berried, or fruiting, ivy too is very useful from September to February, and it is one of the foliages I most miss when I am working in a country that does not have such an abundant supply.

RIGHT A festive swag makes a change from a door wreath, and is just as effective. You need a good assortment of evergreens to give texture and colour as well as shape. Trailing ivy extends outside the boundaries of the design, and gives a sense of flow.

THIS PAGE The density of ivy foliage in this oval table arrangement gives a very natural feel. The flowers include white *Ranunculus* 'Ranobelle Inra Wit', 'Madame Florent Stepman' lilac, 'Winterberg' tulips, Alexis and Avalanche+ roses and *Viburnum opulus*. *Hamamelis virginiana*, or witchhazel, is used to supplement the trails of *Hedera helix* and fruiting ivy.

Fruits and vegetables

In London the fruit markets and flower markets are linked, and so I have always loved turning to the fruit market for some inspiration in the winter when flowers are more expensive. Adding fruit and vegetables to arrangements makes them colourful and textural and costs less than using flowers. So for large designs or to make a budget go further, they are ideal. The idea is not new – the Dutch master painters were doing this in the 17th century – but it works, looks classical and is fun for parties and weddings. Remember that fruit and vegetables give off ethylene gas, which is the grim reaper for flowers, and so they should only be used for events and not for longevity. Christmas time, when the temperatures are lower and when you are using more greenery, is also a good time to experiment.

OPPOSITE A mossed wreath is first lined with ivy berries and red skimmia, then groups of Aqua! roses, gloriosa lilies, dark Colandro roses, 'Mistique' and 'Serena' gerberas, baby aubergines, limes and yellow peppers are wired into the frame.

RIGHT To create this fruited topiary, impale a grapefruit onto the top of a bamboo pole that has been secured into a heavy pot filled with florists' foam. Cover the whole of the grapefruit with strawberries using knotted bamboo picks.

THIS PAGE Fruit can work in formal arrangements for special events. Here, late garden roses have been given an autumnal twist with rose hips, ornamental kales, grasses and ivies. Small apples, groups of kumquats and bunches of grapes add colour and texture.

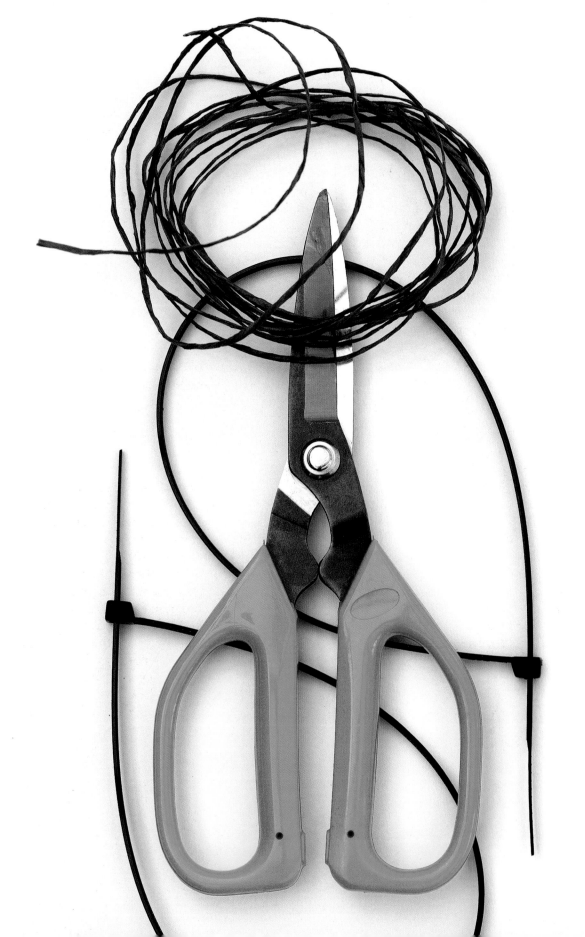

Tools and equipment

For flower arranging and making hand-tied bouquets

The basic tools you need to get started are a good sharp knife and a strong pair of scissors. Generally I find the best tools for the job, including secateurs, tend to be made in Japan. A plastic plant stripper is very useful for stripping stems and removing leaves. A roll of bind wire is my preferred tie: this has a wire running through the centre but is protected by paper so it does not damage the stems.

Flower food for conditioning stems is invaluable, and I also like to have some professional bucket cleaner. A range of vases is required to make the best arrangements, and for hand-tied bouquets bulbous bowls allow the spiral of the stems to sit well in the vase. Thin green florist tape or the new see-through clear rolls are also essential. A range of watering cans and cleaning brushes will prove useful.

For larger designs and floral decorating

Before floral foam was invented moss and chicken wire were the mainstay of the floral decorator. For arches around doors, columns in ceremonies and for huge topiaries, this is still our preferred construction method. We fill 2-5cm (1-inch) chicken wire with damp moss and fashion it into the shape we require. Then we add the foliage and finally the flowers. Sometimes these are wired and sometimes they are be placed in water tubes before pushing them into the moss. Plastic ground sheets and dust sheets should also be part of your essential site-kit to protect flooring and furniture.

Floral foam appeared in the middle of the 20th century and was discovered as a by-product of the Firestone Tyre factory. This revolutionized floristry. It made it easier to make arrangements, and it made it really easy to deliver arrangements. A whole range of shapes was created for the sympathy market, as well as jumbo blocks for big arrangements and designer board for flower walls and specialist one-dimensional designs. For event work, we use a lot of raquettes, caged blocks of foam. Recently some florists have been taking an ethical stance on floral foam, as it is not biodegradable. Water sprays and some flower food sprays are also useful for keeping event flowers fresh.

Structures, columns, hanging decorations and installations

Working out the mechanics is a very important part of the job. It is important that any statement piece or arrangement you create is well designed and stable. I have used carpenters, blacksmiths and fabricators to make frames or arches, to which I can then attach foam and flowers. In time you end up with a good selection of ladders, trolleys, brooms, etc. Double-sided tape, heavy gaffer tape and cable ties in a selection of sizes should also accompany your stub wires and reel wires.

Floristry and wiring

Wiring greenery and flowers into bespoke shapes is the work of a true florist. Real floristry requires a range of wires in a variety of sizes, as well as green and white gutta percha tape for taping wires, and some silver reel wires. A water spray or a Glory spray made by flower food manufacturers Chrysal is helpful for keeping tender wired flowers hydrated.

For wedding work the wires should be as light as possible for the job, and you will also need some pins and ribbons to finish off bouquets and for buttonholes. At present it is very popular to add string, raffia or other decorations to buttonholes to embellish them.

For winter floristry – the garlands, swags and wreaths for the festive season – you will need heavy stub wires and heavy reel wires for binding winter foliage and for adding decoration. In the UK we use a lot of sphagnum moss on frames to make huge wreaths, or you can use twig or straw bases. Disposable gloves or thin gardening gloves are advised at this time of year as Pine and Spruce can be an irritant to skin. The white milky sap from the *Euphorbia* family, such as the poinsettia, can also irritate skin – take care not to rub your eyes as this can be very dangerous. Use a saline solution to wash the eye and contact a doctor if inflamed. Kebab sticks, bamboo skewers and bamboo garden canes are useful for heavier fruits and vegetables and for inserting into the hollow stem of cut amaryllis. Spray paints add sparkle to your festive decorations, and a hot glue gun is useful for attaching nuts and spices onto your decorative designs.

Index

Acknowledgements

This beautiful book, which is my 18th, has been created with a fantastic team of talented people. Thanks to Polly Eltes for the wonderful photography for this new title. Polly was a dream to work with and I am grateful to her and her assistant Ryan Robinson.

Thanks also to the other talented photographers I have had the pleasure to work with in the past: Polly Wreford, Tim Winter, Rachel Whiting, Sian Irvine, Sarah Cuttle and Graham Atkins-Hughes.

Grateful thanks to Jacqui Small of Quarto publishing for her loyal support and 23 years of publishing my books. Thanks also to Charles Miers at Rizzoli in the US for publishing my books for over two decades.

I am also grateful to the Jacqui Small LLP staff for all their support with the book, including Emma Heyworth-Dunn and Joe Hallsworth. Thanks to Liz Somers for her support and enthusiasm for my books.

The two heroines of this project, though, are Maggie Town, my creative Art Director, for the gorgeous design and Sian Parkhouse, my long-standing and very patient editor. It is always a pleasure to work with this team and my heartfelt thanks to both of them for working so hard with such a tight deadline with good grace and fortitude.

The Paula Pryke team
www.paulapryke.com
I am particularly grateful to Hisako Watanabe and Agnieszka Szyc for the support with this title and the rest of the team: Daniel Atkinson, Marta Bialozyt, Wendy Boileau, Anne Cadle, Anita Everard, Tania Newman, Penny Pizey, Jamie Price, Emma Vere-Hodge, Karen Weller.

I have to thank my **suppliers** in Covent Garden market, Dennis Edwards, Pratleys, S R Allen, Porters, GBH Foliage, Best, Whittingtons. My Dutch suppliers: Kees Ros from Select (www.selectflowers.nl) and Marcel Van Eijsden from MHG flowers (www.mhgflowers.com).

The wonderful **growers** in the UK and in Holland: Meijer Roses, VIP Roses, Holstein Gerberas, Gerbera Unlimited and too many more to mention. Grateful thanks to the people who invent the flowers, tend them, care for them 24 hours a day and then cut them and sell them for their onward journey. You are the hardworking heros of the flower world!

Massive thanks is due to a wholesaler local to me in Suffolk
www.trianglenursery.co.uk

Props and vases
www.thelibracompany.co.uk
www.chiveuk.com
www.serax.com
www.despots.nl
www.centuryd.com
www.cravtoriginal.com
www.lsa-international.com
www.cbest.co.uk

Thanks to all the **venues and the locations** in this book:
www.gaynespark.co.uk
www.fetchampark.co.uk
www.thejockeyclub.co.uk
are three of my own personal favourites, as they are run by people passionate about their industry.

Our most humble thanks to all my wonderful **clients**, the ultimate source of our passion, creativity and livelihood.

Photography credits
Page 22 *A Vase of Flowers*, 1663 (oil on canvas), Aelst, Willem van (1626-83) / Ashmolean Museum, University of Oxford, UK / Bridgeman Images

page 24 *Sunflowers*, 1889 (oil on canvas), Gogh, Vincent van (1853-90) / Seiji Togo Memorial Sompo Japan Nipponkoa Museum of Art, Tokyo, Japan / Bridgeman Images

page 30 *Subliminal Yellow Cross*, 1986 (acrylic on wood), McClure, Peter / Private Collection / Bridgeman Images

Page 12 Anne Romaniuk
Pages 19, 20 Paula Pryke

All other photography is copyright © Jacqui Small LLP:

Graham Atkins-Hughes: Page 26

Sarah Cuttle: Pages 49, 52, 53, 59, 70, 71, 82 (bottom row second from left), 83 (top row second from right, bottom row second from left, second from right), 90 (top row second from left, bottom row far left), 91 (top row second from right, far right, bottom row second from right), 92, 95 (top row second from right, bottom row second from left), 99 (top row second from left, second from right, bottom row second from left, far right), 101, 102 (top row second from right, far right, bottom row second from right, far right), 103 (top row second from right, far right, bottom row far left, second from right, far right), 104, 105, 109 (nos. 3, 5), 113 (nos. 1, 3, 4, 5, 8, 9), 115, 119, 121 (no. 6), 125 (nos. 1, 2, 4, 7), 129 (nos. 2, 4, 5, 6, 7, 8), 135 (no. 8), 136, 137, 148, 149, 175, 183, 188, 193, 199, 208, 220, 221, 234, 246, 247, 253, 278

Polly Eltes: Pages 1–7, 11, 13–18, 25, 27–29, 31–41, 60–61, 66, 67, 69, 74, 75, 80, 83 (top row second from left), 89, 94 (bottom row second from right), 96, 97, 111, 122, 123, 126, 130, 131, 138, 139, 141, 190, 191, 212, 213, 224–27, 229, 230–31, 235, 248–251, 267–69, 271

Sian Irvine: Pages 21, 23, 68, 73, 82 (bottom row far right), 83 (bottom row far right), 90 (bottom row second from left), 91 (bottom row far right), 95 (bottom row far right), 99 (top row far left, bottom row far left), 102 (top row far left second from left), 103 (top row second from left), 129 (no. 9), 133, 135 (nos. 3, 5, 6, 9), 144, 145, 152, 160, 161, 163, 180, 196–98, 210, 211, 232, 240, 241, 252, 254, 257, 276, 277

Rachel Whiting: Pages 10, 45, 47, 56, 57, 63, 64, 76, 77, 82 (top row far left, second from left, far right, bottom row far left, second from right), 90 (top row far left, second from right, far right, bottom row far right), 91 (top row far left), 93, 94 (top row far left, second from left, far right, bottom row far left, second from left, far right), 95 (top row far left, second from left, bottom row far left, second from right), 98 (all), 99 (top row far right), 100, 103 (top row far left), 106, 109 (nos. 1, 2, 4, 6, 7), 110, 113 (no. 7), 114, 121 (nos. 3, 4, 5, 9), 125 (nos. 3, 5, 6, 8, 9), 127, 129 (nos. 1, 3), 132, 135 (nos. 1, 2, 4, 7), 140, 146, 156, 157, 168, 181, 200–205, 214, 218, 219, 222, 242–45, 256, 258, 260, 261–66, 270, 272–75

Tim Winter: Pages 8, 9, 42–44, 51, 54, 55,, 62, 79, 82 (top row second from right), 83 (top row far left, far right, bottom row far left), 84, 85, 90 (bottom row second from right), 91 (top row second from left, bottom row far left, second from left), 94 (top row second from right), 95 (top row far right), 99 (bottom row second from right), 103 (bottom row second from left), 109 (no. 9), 113 (nos. 2, 6), 118, 121 (nos. 1, 2, 7), 147, 153, 158, 159, 164–67, 170–74, 176–79, 182, 194, 209, 216, 217, 228, 233, 236–39, 255, 279–82

Polly Wreford: Pages 58, 65, 72, 78, 88, 102 (bottom row far left, second from left), 109 (no. 8), 121 (no. 8), 142, 150, 151, 154, 155, 162, 184, 186, 187, 189, 192, 195, 206, 207, 223